P9-CLF-654

Geoffrey Chaucer, *Second Edition*

Twayne's English Authors Series

George D. Economou, Editor

University of Oklahoma

TEAS 1

Portrait of Chaucer from the Ellesmere MS of the Canterbury Tales, *El 26 C 9, folio 153v. Reproduced by permission of the Huntington Library, San Marino, California.*

Geoffrey Chaucer, *Second Edition*

By Robert O. Payne

City University of New York

Twayne Publishers • Boston

Geoffrey Chaucer, Second Edition

Robert O. Payne

Published by Twayne Publishers
A Division of G.K. Hall & Co.
70 Lincoln Street
Boston, Massachusetts 02111

Copyediting supervised by Lewis DeSimone
Book production by Elizabeth Todesco
Book design by Barbara Anderson

Typeset in 11 pt. Garamond
by P&M Typesetting, Inc., Waterbury, Connecticut

Printed on permanent/durable acid-free paper
and bound in the United States of America

Library of Congress Cataloging in Publication Data

Payne, Robert O.
Geoffrey Chaucer.

(Twayne's English authors series; TEAS 1)
Bibliography: p. 143
Includes index.
1. Chaucer, Geoffrey, d. 1400—Criticism and interpretation.
I. Title. II. Series.
PR1924.P347 1986 821'.1 85-16368
ISBN 0-8057-6908-0

Contents

About the Author

Robert O. Payne is a graduate of the University of Oregon (A.B., 1948) and the Johns Hopkins University (A.M., 1951; Ph.D., 1953). He is a member of Phi Beta Kappa and held a President's Fund Scholarship during his graduate study at Johns Hopkins. In 1951 he was appointed instructor in English at the University of Cincinnati and taught there for the following thirteen years, with interludes in Europe on sabbatical leave in 1958–59 and as a visiting professor at the University of Washington, Seattle, in 1962–63. In 1964 he was appointed professor of English at the University of Washington, where he served until 1972. In the summer of 1967, he was visiting professor at the University of Arizona. Since 1972, he has been professor of English at Herbert H. Lehman College and the Graduate Center, City University of New York. He is a member of the Modern Language Association of America (president of its Chaucer Group in 1964), the Medieval Academy of America, and the New Chaucer Society. His previous publications include *The Key of Remembrance: A Study of Chaucer's Poetics* (1963) and several articles, mostly concerned with the relationships between Chaucer's poetry and medieval theories of literature. Recently he has become involved, along with other members of the Chaucer Group of the Modern Language Association, in some experiments in reading Chaucer's poetry aloud in Middle English—a project that may lead to the publication of some tape recordings.

Preface

This book is addressed not to beginners in the serious study of literature, but to beginners in the close and careful study of Chaucer's poetry. In assuming such readers, I also assume that most of them are probably seriously confronting, for the first time, medieval literature and the world out of which it grew. I have therefore tried to organize these discussions so that readers may see Chaucer's poetry in its own right and for its own artistic values, but also as it developed from the context of late medieval European literary traditions and practices, with which Chaucer was widely and deeply acquainted.

Because Chaucer's work reflects so little of his personal and professional life, and because little of it mirrors directly the fourteenth century he knew well, I have devoted only one relatively short chapter to his life and times. Recent generations of Chaucer scholars, however, have produced several excellent, highly readable, and relatively brief surveys of Chaucer's life, his public career, and his late medieval cultural milieu. I have listed several of the best of these studies in the bibliography. For nearly all the factual material in the opening chapter, I am dependent upon the *Chaucer Life Records,* edited by Martin M. Crow and Clair C. Olson. That marvelous compendium of all the surviving fourteenth-century documents that bear witness to Chaucer's life and work (and some other relevant material as well) may at first intimidate a beginner, but it is abundantly supplied with summaries and translations of key Latin and Anglo-French passages. Browsing through this material offers one a wonderful feeling for the nuts and bolts and working machinery of fourteenth-century middle- and upper-class society.

One feature of Chaucer's cultural equipment—one absolutely fundamental to his writing—I have chosen not to discuss in this general survey, namely, the London dialect of Middle English in which he wrote. Except for some brief remarks in chapter 1 and some indirect considerations in a later discussion of his meters and stanza forms, readers will find in this book no introduction to the linguistic history or to the details of sound, vocabulary, and structure of Chaucer's English. That is partly because modern scholarship has provided the interested beginner with good, reliable, detailed introductions to fourteenth-century English. But it is mainly because a thorough study of linguistic matters requires a treatment that could not be provided in a book of this length.

I have tried to give readers a sense of the overall shape of the over-thirty-year career of one of our greatest writers, a career as distinguished for variety, experimentation, and imaginative manipulation of received traditions as it is for overwhelming individual successes like *Troilus and Criseyde* and the *Canterbury Tales*. It may well be that the hardest thing for a modern reader of Chaucer is to imagine the extent to which, as a writer, he lived at the leading edge of his times, deeply rooted in a high-medieval academic Latin tradition, but equally knowledgeable in avant-garde contemporary French and Italian art and ideas that, by Chaucer's death in 1400, had only just begun to affect most of his English contemporaries.

A consequence of this effort is that the second chapter of this book is a description and interpretation of the principal theories of literature—most but not all of them academic theories—of Chaucer's time, and of the two preceding centuries. It is fairly easy to show that Chaucer had some direct familiarity with several of the writings that embody these ideas; it is harder (but more fun) to make out his responses to them and the degrees to which, positively or negatively, they influenced the ways in which he wrote. But perhaps the most interesting and hardest of all is to consider that the various and sometimes contradictory things people had been thinking and saying about writing for generations before he was born must in some confused and subliminal way have defined what he thought he was doing when he, the schoolboy Geoffrey Chaucer, first thought "I'm going to write a poem." However vague or unarticulated it may be, a cultural matrix is a very real thing. A school child in the 1980s who says "I'm going to be a ballet dancer" or "I'm going to be a quarterback" or (more unlikely) "I'm going to be a poet" is expressing a perception of distinctions and definitions as much indigenous to current American culture as they are expressions of the child's own specific tastes and talents, although he or she probably could not articulate either of them with any precision or with a bibliography of sources.

Unlike most of us who make such school-age wish assertions, the Geoffrey Chaucer who must once have said for the first time "I'm going to write a poem" did eventually write several of the best in our language. And as he worked and learned to do so, that vague, subconscious cultural matrix crystallized into an ever-enlarging body of specific books read, of writers considered and agreed or disagreed with, and of poems admired and imitated, revered from afar, or scorned and satirized—or some characteristically Chaucerian mixture of all these.

My third chapter considers, briefly and generally, the major works of Latin, French, and Italian literature (he seems to have been very little impressed with his predecessors in English) that Chaucer knew and loved and drew upon heavily throughout his career. In this chapter I offer an introductory guide into a complex area of knowledge that modern scholarship is constantly enlarging, but it is also an area the general map of which has long been known and which every reader of Chaucer must enter almost immediately, for there have been few writers so insistent as he was that we recognize and acknowledge the earlier writers he read, loved, and took so much from.

Against this general background, I try in the subsequent chapters to do two things more or less simultaneously but by different means. First, in the arrangement of chapters and in the materials discussed in them, I want to convey not the simple chronology (which in any case is nearly impossible to establish), but my sense of the overall shape and direction of Chaucer's poetic career: the problems he tried to solve, the varying periods of concentration on specific issues, and his unfailing concern for his art and for himself as practitioner of it. Second, I offer for each of Chaucer's major poems a discussion intended both to present my own reading, response to, and evaluation of each, and to incite, as much as I can, the reader's own responses and evaluations, given the tools and suggestions my chapters contribute.

The transitional chapter in this scheme, chapter 4, requires a brief additional comment. In it, I may have slighted some excellent poetry among the not large body of work Chaucer left us. But in grouping together all the short "lyric" pieces scattered throughout his thirty-odd years of writing, I have simply made an arbitrary procedural decision. None of the work on which Chaucer's reputation rests is among these poems, but a basic stylistic quality of his greatness is easily discernible in them: the development of his skill as a metrist and his constant experimentation with prosodic and stanzaic forms. I suspect that a major reason for his reputation, from early times, as a convincing "realistic" observer and conveyer of his world is that his verse nearly always sounds right. The forms of his lines and stanzas so aptly organize their contents that, even when he writes conventional banalities, the lines often sound so just, so smoothly worked, that their artificially achieved "naturalness" convinces us that this is indeed the way things were when freshly observed by their author. Consequently, I have taken advantage of these short poems to present a discussion not so much of them as of what they can teach us about Chaucer's constant attention to the basic technical craft of the poet and his ever-increasing mastery of it.

The last three chapters, on the dream-vision poems, *Troilus and Criseyde,* and the *Canterbury Tales,* require little preparatory comment here. They are straightforward attempts to say what I think are the best things in those works, how they make a kind of pattern in Chaucer's career, and what things about them a beginning reader should most attend to. However, it may be as well to set down here what every experienced teacher and scholar knows but what even sophisticated beginners may be troubled by. There is nearly nothing in this book for which I am not indebted, either directly or indirectly, to the work of other readers of Chaucer over most of the six hundred years since his death. Most of this debt I have not tried to acknowledge, because the audience I anticipate does not want to be buried under a mass of footnotes and book lists. I have also tried to avoid initiating or continuing battles with colleagues and predecessors with whom, although I may have learned much from them, I disagree. An attentive reader of this book will often find himself amid controversial issues. My sole intent is to leave him there and wish him well in orienting himself among them. At the same time, I must insist upon the obvious: these pages are a record, a self-evident one I sincerely hope, of a personal response to Chaucer's art and a personal evaluation of it. I do not see how it could be otherwise, and the greatest success I could wish for this book is that readers will be led to a similarly personal involvement with the poems, however different it may be from mine. A relatively recent—and, let us all hope, transient—fashion in the study of medieval literature has been to propose that we must never make our own personal, "modern" responses to it, but rather must pretend to know what some hypothetical fourteenth-century reader would have thought and then try to imitate his supposed responses. That is not only impossible, but also irrelevant to why Chaucer's works have remained vital and lovely for six hundred years. They are, like all great art, works that first of all engage us personally and have that almost magical variety and richness that can elicit a wide range of personal response from a wide range of people. The differences themselves are one kind of measure of the greatness of the poems. But the poems remain, and it is to them that everything in this book is intended to direct attention.

Robert O. Payne

City University of New York

Chronology

1340–1345	Geoffrey Chaucer born in London some time during this period.
1357	Appears in records in service of Elizabeth, countess of Ulster.
1359–1360	In military service with English army in France, captured near Reims, and ransomed by King Edward III.
1366	Travels in Spain. Marries Philippa, daughter of Sir Payne Roet.
1367	Awarded annuity for life by Edward III.
ca. 1370	*Book of the Duchess,* first major poem.
1370–1386	*House of Fame; Parliament of Foules; Troilus and Criseyde; Legend of Good Women.*
1372–1373	First diplomatic mission to Italy.
1374	Appointed comptroller of customs in Port of London. Moves into Aldgate house.
1377	Diplomatic missions in Flanders and France. Richard II becomes king.
1378	Second diplomatic mission to Italy.
1381	Peasant's Rebellion.
1385	Justice of peace in Kent.
1386	Elected knight of the shire for Kent and serves in Parliament.
1387	Philippa Chaucer dies.
1389	Appointed clerk of the king's works.
1391	Appointed deputy forester for the royal forest of North Petherton.
1387–1400	*Canterbury Tales.*
1394	Richard II grants Chaucer new annuity.
1399	Henry IV becomes king and renews Chaucer's annuities and grants.

1399 4 December, Chaucer leases house in Westminster Abbey garden.

1400 25 October, Chaucer dies.

Chapter One
Chaucer's Life

Geoffrey Chaucer was born into the middle of a century that, like most centuries, was crowded with catastrophes, full of violence, socially and economically unstable, and rapidly changing. His London, like its twentieth-century descendant, was an exciting and dangerous city, very much a part of European cultural and economic life, though at the same time somewhat remote from the principal continental metropolises and in many ways distinctly English. And the family into which Geoffrey was born was especially fortunately placed to permit him to grow up aware and perceptive of the rich cosmopolitan variety of his time and place.

The Chaucers had, for three generations before Geoffrey's birth, been steadily coming up in the world. Although the name itself, from the French *chaussier,* would seem to indicate a connection with making or trading in shoes or hose, the earliest surviving records show that Geoffrey's great-grandfather was a wine merchant in Ipswich, and the family stayed in the wine trade until Geoffrey's time. To anyone unfamiliar with late medieval customs, the names here may seem puzzling, but in fourteenth-century England the modern pattern of a given name (or names) and a fixed family surname had not yet crystallized as universal practice. Geoffrey Chaucer's great-grandfather appears in contemporary records as Andrew de Dinnington, of the small port city of Ipswich, northeast of London. Since he also appears sometimes as Andrew le Taverner, he was unmistakably in the wine business, although the word *taverner* need not necessarily imply that he merely operated a bar.

Andrew's son Robert (Geoffrey's grandfather) was apparently the first to use the name Chaucer. He appears in records under various names (as was not uncommon then), including Robert de Dinnington, Robert Malin, Robert Malin le Chaucer, and Robert le Chaucer. He was a man of considerable substance in Ipswich. He owned valuable property, and according to Ipswich corporation records was in the king's service as early as 1305. It was he who moved to London, and he may have taken his "shoemaker" name because he settled in the Cordwainer's Street district—"cordwainer" being a version of "cordovan," the valuable imported leather that was one of the staples of business in the district. He may in fact have had something to do with the leather trade, for he appears in one document as Robert le Saddler.

Whatever the year-by-year details, the Chaucer family was clearly on the move from lower middle class in a small city to upper middle class in a large one. As their fortunes improved, they acquired a variety of business and property interests, with the inevitable family squabbles over money and property occasionally breaking out into lawsuits and court actions still preserved in the records. People in the fourteenth century were no less litigious than they are today, and fourteenth-century lawyers no less eager to scavenge off their litigation than those of our time. It is also entirely probable that some thin-skinned nouveau-riche pride was involved, especially in a society whose new bourgeoisie was thrusting itself uncertainly into power and prominence as the old hierarchies of wealth and power were collapsing and as what we would now call commercial capitalism was being born.

Geoffrey's father, John, born to Robert and Mary Chaucer in London in 1312 or 1313, was himself caught up in one of those family controversies while still in his early teens. After his father's death and his mother's remarriage to a Richard Chaucer (about whom we know nothing more), John was forcibly kidnapped by his aunt Agnes and some Ipswich co-conspirators with the intention of securing the property of the London Chaucers by a shotgun wedding of John to his cousin Joan, Agnes's daughter. A group of John's London relatives, however, rescued the boy, and Agnes and her cohorts eventually served a jail sentence and paid a heavy fine.

Having avoided that early pitfall, John Chaucer survived an adventurous and occasionally dangerous early manhood, took over, and considerably expanded, the family's London holdings. His nearest brush with disaster came in 1329, and it too tells us a good deal about the world into which Geoffrey was born.

In 1328, Queen Isabella and her lover Roger Mortimer had murdered King Edward II and assumed control of the realm. But Isabella and Mortimer were even more widely hated—and certainly more widely feared—than Edward had been, and the earl of Lancaster led a rebellion against them in 1329. The rest of the century was punctuated with alarming frequency by such plots, insurrections, usurpations, and various riots, but in this instance John Chaucer (unlike his son Geoffrey, who developed an uncanny ability to come through such things untouched) joined the wrong side. He enlisted in support of Lancaster, and when the rebellion failed, he was indicted for his participation. Having the good sense not to appear for trial, he was outlawed, which was certainly preferable to the hanging, drawing, and quartering he could very likely have been sentenced to had he stood trial.

By 1330, however, the young King Edward III had taken control of things for himself. Isabella's power was broken, Mortimer executed, and Henry of Lancaster's faction pardoned. From about 1337 to his death in 1366 we can trace John Chaucer through the public records as he develops into a wealthy, influential, and well-connected London businessman, a type that, however maligned by social satirists of more recent times, was indeed the pillar of the kingdom in the turbulent and nearly catastrophic fourteenth and fifteenth centuries. John Chaucer continued in the family tradition as a vintner and also dealt successfully in London real estate as well as investing in some shops. In addition, he maintained and strengthened the family's connection with the royal service, being appointed in 1347 to the important post of deputy butler for the collection of customs from foreign merchants in Southampton.

A document dated 19 October refers to John Chaucer and his wife, Agnes. Although we cannot recover the date of their marriage (it must have been several years earlier), other records identify her as a daughter of John de Copton, and as such a part of a wealthy and influential Kentish family. What we should like most to know about this prosperous, busy important London couple in the 1340s, however, seems to be irretrievably lost: the exact birthdate of their son Geoffrey. Years later, in 1386, when he appeared as a witness for one party in a lawsuit, he was entered in the court record as "Geffray Chaucere esquier del age xl ans et plus armeez par xxvii ans . . ." (Geoffrey Chaucer, esquire, more than forty years old and having borne arms for twenty-seven years).[1] Neither figure tells us anything precise, but if he, like most young aristocrats of his time, first put on a sword and joined in a military venture at fourteen or fifteen, and if the "more than forty years" means not much beyond, then the two dates seem to agree in implying a birthdate not much before 1345. Most modern scholars hedge their bets by placing Geoffrey's birth somewhere between 1340 and 1345. Of other children of John and Agnes, we know only of a Catherine, mentioned in a later marriage record as "sister of Geoffrey Chaucer, knight, celebrated among English poets."

It seems safe to assume that Geoffrey was born and grew up in the house his parents owned in the Vintry district, a prosperous and fashionable London neighborhood peopled mostly by well-to-do merchant-importers and frequented by the aristocracy and even by some of the royal family, with which many of the residents had business and political connections. This house stood in Thames Street, a street paralleling the river, whose residents had only a couple of blocks' walk to the piers and docks where the goods they dealt in, mainly wines, were loaded and unloaded. In 1381, "Geoffrey Chaucer, son of John Chaucer, Vintner of London," deeded away the interest he had inherited in this property, and the document describes it as "situated in the parish of St. Martins, in the Vintry of London, between the dwellings of William Gager on the east and John Mazeliner on the west and . . . from Thames Street on the south to Wallbrook on the north. . . ."

Although many traces of the fourteenth-century London that Chaucer knew remain today, the whole Thames Street area where he grew up was leveled by German bombers during World War II. John and Agnes's house had doubtless disappeared before that. We can guess generally that the Chaucers lived comfortably and that Geoffrey grew up in a cosmopolitan, active, relatively safe part of the city, probably acquainted from early on with the wealthy and well-born, the movers and shakers of fourteenth-century London.

There were several notable schools in the district and, though we have no written evidence, tradition has long had it that young Geoffrey attended St. Paul's Almonry School, widely known and highly regarded for centuries after Chaucer's time. For us who grew up in the twentieth century, it is easy to see medieval schools as harsh, austere, and terribly intellectually narrow. Yet they produced many men of real learning and warm humaneness, from the fruits of whose intellectual efforts we still benefit. Geoffrey Chaucer is an excellent case in point. Whatever the schoolmasters of St. Paul's did to and for the schoolboy Geoffrey, he carried away from them a lifelong love of books and learning—scientific as well as literary—all the more impressive when we take into account that he was neither clergyman nor academic, but a practical man of affairs whose pleasure in the life of the mind must have been largely self-motivated and self-propelled.

In any case, Chaucer's upbringing in the household of a prominent Vintry merchant with good social and political connections also placed him well in line for another, perhaps equally important kind of education open to well-endowed children of the upper middle class and lower aristocracy. By June 1356—he was then just into his teens, somewhere between eleven and fifteen—he had been placed in the service of Elizabeth, countess of Ulster, wife of Lionel, duke of Clarence, the third child of King Edward III. Undoubtedly John and Agnes Chaucer, like many of their equally well-placed contemporaries, had mixed motives for placing their promising son in such service. It surely was to the parents' advantage to establish a close connection with the court, but it also gave the boy a chance for a marvelous first-hand experience of courtly life and manners, a good deal of first-class travel, and an introduction to the political maneuvering and tightrope walking that would prove invaluable in the forty-four-year career of high public service that he was to give his king and country.

The few surviving pages of the Countess Elizabeth's household accounts list various payments to Geoffrey Chaucer for travel expenses, good clothes, holiday treats, etc., all between 1356 and 1359, but nowhere is it recorded exactly what kind of position he held on her staff or what his specified duties were. From our point of view, what must have been most important was his opportunity to observe courtly life and society, all of which was to become an integral part of the great poetry we remember him for. From his own point of view, perhaps his greatest and most productive duty was to win the approval and learn to serve well a royal family that was to insure his career for the rest of his life. And an interested reader of those otherwise dull-looking columns of the household budget will also note that during Geoffrey's period of service, one of the group of lively and lovely girls also attending upon Elizabeth was Philippa Pan, daughter of the Flemish knight Sir Payne de Roet; by September 1366, she had become Philippa Chaucer, Geoffrey's wife.

It is usual nowadays to assume that Geoffrey was a page of some sort to the Countess; if so, he probably traveled considerably during those three years:

> usually from one royal residence to another, visiting Reading, Stratford, Campsey, London, Windsor, Woodstock, Doncaster, Hatfield, Angelsey, Bristol, and Liverpool. He would have witnessed the preparations for such festivals as Easter (in London), Christmas (at Hatfield), and Epiphany (at Bristol). He would have observed the Countess's preparations for the be-

trothal of her infant daughter Phillippa to Edmund Mortimer, Earl of March. He might have been present at the funeral of Queen Isabella (in London 27 November 1358). More exciting would have been a visit to see the lions in the tower of London and tournaments at Smithfield, for which the Countess had prepared cushions of tapestry.[2]

By late 1359 Chaucer had moved out of the countess's household service and into that of her husband, Lionel, to participate in one of the endless series of inconclusive military campaigns in France that marked the Hundred Years' War—a futile effort to unite the crowns of France and England. Perhaps this was the first time the young bourgeois-aspiring-to-be-courtier bore the arms that he later swore to having taken up at about this time. We know little about what he did on that campaign, save that in a skirmish along the way he was captured by the French, probably an indication that he was recognized as having some status, otherwise no one would have bothered to hold him for ransom. On 1 March 1360, a £16 ransom was paid out of King Edward III's own accounts for "Galfrido Chaucer capto par inimicos in partibus Francie in subsidium redempcionis sue" (Geoffrey Chaucer, captured by enemies in French territory, in payment of his ransom). Late Victorian Chaucer scholars used to give themselves schoolmasterly chuckles by noting that at the time, £16 was about the price of a good horse.

Thus, in his mid or late teens, which by fourteenth-century standards was the threshold of responsible adulthood, Chaucer probably had behind him a solid fundamental academic education at St. Paul's school, an extensive social one in Elizabeth's household, and the beginnings of a military and political one in Lionel's service, where he had in some way also drawn King Edward's attention. It has even been suggested by some modern scholars that the 1359–60 winter campaign with the duke of Clarence in France may have given the young man his first contact with the exciting new poetry of contemporary Frenchmen, especially Eustache Deschamps, Guillaume de Machaut, and Jean Froissart. This could have been the case, but the assumption is hardly necessary, because Chaucer almost certainly grew up speaking both French and English, like most well-bred young men of his day, and given his developing literary interests, would have discovered their work soon had he never visited France.

But just here, with predictably frustrating capriciousness, the historical record turns up blank. For the next six or seven years, presumably an enormously important period in Chaucer's life, we have no trace of him. By the time his name appears in the court records again, in April 1367, he is in the household of King Edward III (referred to as "our beloved valet"); he has already married Philippa (Pan) Roet (other documents indicate a marriage date in 1366); he has, according to recently recognized evidence, returned from an expedition into Spain with Edward the Black Prince; and he has established some kind of relationship with John of Gaunt, duke of Lancaster, close enough that within a couple of years Chaucer will write his first major poem on the occasion of the death of John's wife, Blanche.

Scholars of the past have tended to fill in this gap with a variety of speculations. One of the more likely is that Chaucer may have spent some time studying law at the Inns of Court, a famous fourteenth-century experiment in education that for the first time in medieval Europe offered legal—and considerable general—education to young men not in clerical orders. And it is true that throughout his career as a public servant, Chaucer held positions that required considerable acquaintance with the complexities and technicalities of medieval law (and one of the Canterbury pilgrims is a sergeant of law). Still, the only evidence (if it is evidence at all) is a claim by Thomas Speght, in a life of Chaucer written in 1598, two hundred years after Chaucer's death, that "not many yeeres since, Master Buckley did see a Record in [the Inner Temple of the Inns of Court] where Geoffrey Chaucer was fined two shillings for beating a Franciscane fryer in Fleetestreete."

Among the less likely conjectures are a number of variously improbable love affairs, even including a startlingly improbable one with Blanche, duchess of Lancaster. What little we actually know about the sex lives of young men in the court circles Geoffrey was then traveling in makes it unlikely that he diligently preserved a monastic chastity. But nowhere in his writing does he ever, even obliquely, give us hints about his private life, either during the 1360s or subsequently during the years of his marriage to Philippa. It is true that more than twenty years later he was involved in an unpleasant affair with a woman named Cecily Champaign, who in May 1380 filed in court a release of "Geoffrey Chaucer, knight, from any kind of action concerning my rape"; but the scanty and confusing court record makes it impossible for us to understand precisely what happened.

Whatever he was doing during most of the 1360s—and we shall probably never know—Chaucer emerges again into the daylight of preserved public records at the end of the decade, and for the remaining thirty-odd years of his life we can follow him in considerable detail through a busy and productive career in the service of three successive monarchs, in service abroad, in England, and in the City of London. With less clarity and with far less direct evidence outside the surviving fifteenth-century manuscript copies, we can also follow him through the composition, from the *Book of the Duchess* through the *Canterbury Tales,* of a body of work that made him the dominant influence in English poetry for the next two centuries and ranks him, with Spenser, Shakespeare, and Milton, among the greatest writers England has produced.

Although several documents from the late 1360s and early 1370s show Chaucer in increasingly important occupations in the service of King Edward III, he was forming perhaps an even more important connection during those years with Edward's third son, John of Gaunt, duke of Lancaster. Like so many things about Geoffrey Chaucer, the exact nature of his relationship with the duke eludes our modern attempts to fill in between the raw facts of a scanty and scattered but always suggestive public record.

The connection seems to have been established by 1368, when Lancaster's first wife, the rich and beautiful Blanche, died. She was a daughter of the same Henry of Lancaster whom Chaucer's father had served in a lost and nearly disastrous cause, and it was John of Gaunt's marriage to her that brought him the land and title of Lancaster. Chaucer commemorated her death in what seems to be his first major poem, the *Book of the Duchess,* probably written not long after she died, although we have no certain means of dating it precisely. No one knows whether Chaucer wrote it at the duke's request, or whether he wrote it on his own to increase his favor with Lancaster, whom he may already have served in some capacity on a 1369 military expedition into northern France. Some modern Chaucerians continue to refer to John of Gaunt as Chaucer's "patron," but the term may be misleading. Ordinarily, a patron provides an artist with a livelihood in order to support his artistic production, and nothing now known indicates that the duke ever did any such thing for Chaucer. In 1374, he granted a £10 annuity for life, in consideration of "la bone et agreable service que nostre bien ame Geffray Chaucer nous ad fait et auxint pur la bone service que nostre bien ame Phillipe sa femme ad fait a nostre treshonure dame et miere la royne que Dieu pardoigne et a nostre tres ame compaigne la royne de Castille . . ."

(the good and agreeable service that our good friend Geoffrey Chaucer has done us and also for the good service that our good friend Philippa his wife has done for our honored mother the queen, whom may God pardon, and to our beloved companion the queen of Castille . . .). The second queen mentioned was Lancaster's second wife, Constance of Castille, in whose household Philippa had served. The phrasing seems to refer unmistakably to personal, political, or military services—not to the support of the career of a rising young writer.

Still, there must have been more to it than that. Katherine Roet Swynford, Lancaster's mistress for many years and eventually his third wife, was a sister of Philippa Chaucer. The duke must have had a hand in some of Chaucer's political appointments during his career, although again we have to note that not infrequently Chaucer aligned himself with factions opposed to the Lancastrians in London city affairs and in Parliament. Perhaps fourteenth-century politics were not quite so utterly cutthroat as they sometimes appear to be. In any case, Lancaster's eldest son, Henry, earl of Derby, made two modest grants to Chaucer in 1395 and 1396, and then after usurping the throne from Richard II and becoming King Henry IV, renewed and increased Chaucer's annuities, although by that time the aging poet and public servant was to have only about a year of life left in which to enjoy them.

Another association that has intrigued modern scholars is that during the thirty or so years of Chaucer's acquaintance with John of Gaunt, the duke was also the friend and protector of that fierce and austere religious reformer John Wycliffe. We have nothing to confirm a direct relationship between Chaucer and Wycliffe, and Chaucer certainly had little in common with the stiff-necked, opinionated, often dogmatic attacker of clerical corruption and church bureaucracy. Yet, perhaps through the duke of Lancaster, Chaucer surely knew about Wycliffe and the storm he was blowing up in fourteenth-century religious and intellectual life. We have, in fact, a few other scattered indications that Chaucer was acquainted with some of Wycliffe's contemporaries at Oxford. (Indeed, there was a tradition in the sixteenth century, almost certainly wrong, that Chaucer had studied at Oxford.) One of these men, the logician Ralph Strode, who sometimes argued against Wycliffe, even appears in the dedication at the end of Chaucer's *Troilus and Criseyde.* What is important here is the indication that Chaucer had fairly direct contact with one of the major centers of contemporary intellectual life, in addition to his experience of its political and artistic activities.

To return to about 1370, just as the composition of the *Book of the Duchess* signals the beginning of his career as a major poet and confirms the beginning of a lifelong relationship with the powerful house of Lancaster, Chaucer is also notably advancing himself in the service of the king and of the City of London. In 1370 he was issued letters of protection, a medieval form of passport, for "going in the king's service to parts beyond the seas," but the mission seems to have been secret and the record gives us no details. Two years later, however, he was sent on a mission we do know something about, and it was of enormous importance to him, both as poet and as courtier in the crown's service. Together with John de Mari and Sir James de Provan, "Geoffrey Chaucer, King's esquire," was appointed in 1372 to an important commission to negotiate a trade agreement between England and the merchants of Genoa. It was, as far as we know, Chaucer's first trip to Italy, although it is more than likely that part of the reason for his appointment was that his family background in the wine trade and the busy Thames Street district had already given him considerable acquaintance with the language and business practices of the Italians. In any case, for the next ten years or so, in a concentrated burst of poetic activity, Chaucer reflects a deep influence from Boccaccio, Petrarch, and Dante, the dominant Italian poets of the first half of the fourteenth century. It must surely have been his ventures into Italian diplomacy in the 1370s that roused him, so far ahead of other English writers, to this marvelously productive response to the new art of the budding Italian Renaissance.

While Chaucer and his fellow diplomats were negotiating in Genoa, their commission was apparently extended to include a trip to Florence, probably for some dealings with Florentine banking houses. It was another piece of Chaucer's lifelong good luck that fourteenth-century Florence was Italy's premier cultural center, the mother city of many great painters, sculptors, craftsmen, and writers who were generating an artistic efflorescence that would dominate Europe for two or three centuries to come.

The records tell us nothing of the results of this diplomatic mission, but Chaucer's performance must have pleased King Edward, for during the later 1370s Chaucer went back and forth to France several times on the king's business, one of the trips evidently involving negotiations for a marriage (which never came about) of Edward's young grandson and heir apparent, Richard, with Marie, daughter of King Charles V of France.

In 1378, the men in charge of the government during the minority of the newly crowned, eleven-year-old King Richard II sent Chaucer again to Italy, this time for some delicate and secret diplomacy with Barnabo Visconti, lord of Milan, the exact nature of which lies forever buried in the ambiguous court Latin of the commission to one of Chaucer's colleagues, Sir Edward de Berkeley: "pro certis negociis expedicionem guerre tangentibus" (for certain business in connection with a military expedition). In preparation for this journey, Chaucer left a power of attorney with another prominent London poet and man of affairs, John Gower. Although Gower's literary reputation has not held up well in our own time, he was highly regarded in his own, and down through the seventeenth century was generally considered more or less Chaucer's equal, so here again we find Chaucer—now in his middle or late thirties—appearing in close touch with a leading figure of his time.

The decade from the mid-1370s to the mid-1380s was an incredibly busy and productive period in Chaucer's life. In addition to frequent trips to Italy and France in the royal service, he had been appointed in 1374 "controller of the wool custom and wool subsidy and of the petty custom" for the Port of London. Even though during part of his tenure he had a deputy to do much of the work this involved, Chaucer nevertheless remained responsible for the administration of this important governmental agency in the large, busy shipping center. (Incidentally, it is curious that although the commissions of appointment for such positions regularly state that the records are to be kept in the comptroller's own hand, not a scrap of anything known to be Chaucer's handwriting survives today.) By the summer of 1386, he had managed to compose four major poems (though he left two of them unfinished): *The Parliament of Fowls, The House of Fame, Troilus and Criseyde,* and *The Legend of Good Women*. In addition, as he tells us in the Prologue to *The Legend of Good Women,* the last work in this burst of poetic activity, he had translated the great thirteenth-century French poem *Le roman de la rose,* though only part of his translation has been preserved; he began and soon abandoned a poem called *Anelida and Arcite,* based on the Italian Boccaccio's long epic about the siege of Thebes; he wrote a life of Saint Cecelia which subsequently appears as one of the *Canterbury Tales;* he made a prose translation of one of the most influential philosophical treatises of the Middle Ages, Boethius's *Consolation of Philosophy;* and he probably wrote as well several of his surviving short lyric poems.

During most of this decade, Chaucer and his wife, Philippa, lived in comfortable lodgings built (curiously, to us, but not to fourteenth-century Londoners) onto and into the city's wall over its easternmost gate, Aldgate, a little north of the Tower of London. Although he was a busy diplomatic traveler, he spent a good deal of time at home in London, attending to his duties at the port and to other involvements in the city. He must have spent considerable time in this house, which, as generations of Chaucer scholars have felt, gave him incomparable opportunities to observe an ebb and flow of life much different from that of his native Thames Street district. As Crow and Olson describe it in the *Life Records:*

> Even in times of peace Aldgate must have been a busy place, with much traffic going in and out of the city through this portal. The nature of this traffic is described in a document of 1376, appointing a commission to levy twopence a week on every iron-bound cart bringing victuals to the city by way of Aldgate, and every cart and car *(curtena)* bringing blood and entrails of slaughtered beasts entering the city or returning the same way; a penny a week on every cart or car not iron-bound bringing dung, etc.; and a half-penny a week on every horse laden with grain, etc., the money to be expended on the repair of the highway outside Aldgate.[3]

We scarcely need to be reminded how important the lively activity he observed from Aldgate would be to the man who, a few years later, would write the *Canterbury Tales*. It is equally interesting to note that during the last several years of his Aldgate residence Chaucer was writing *Troilus and Criseyde,* a masterpiece that drew equally directly upon his penetrating direct observation of the sophisticated manners and subtle shades of feeling in high court society. Yet one terrifying incident during his Aldgate residence should remind us that Chaucer's new position and growing prominence might have had attendant hazards at least as great as the rewards they brought, even though his shrewdness and good luck kept him from suffering them. For years the old manorial system, which had provided at least a modicum of stability and security to compensate for the wretchedly hard life of the peasants, had been disintegrating. The new commercial capitalism, based largely on the wool trade, had not yet provided much of a labor market as an alternative for the lowest classes. Indeed, the wool men had fueled the anger of the peasants and added an ugly strain of racism to the whole mess by importing skilled and semi-skilled Flemish workers (we would now call them Belgian or Dutch), who were often bitterly resented. And the last straw seems to have been a levy of heavy new taxes by Richard II's government, taxes that a majority defiantly refused to pay.

By June 1381 large and surprisingly well organized bands of infuriated peasants were in open rebellion in the southern counties. On 13 June a large group that had been encamped in the fields of Mile End just outside Aldgate broke in through the gate beneath Chaucer's house and poured into the city, where their previous discipline and organization promptly dissolved in a murderous frenzy of destruction. As the wave of smashing and burning spread westward across the city, Flemings were chased through the streets and brutally butchered when caught. When the rebels came to the Savoy, the gorgeous new palace that John of Gaunt had recently built in the Strand, the street that connected the city with the court and cathedral at Westminster, they set upon it with an especial vengeance, for the duke of Lancaster seems most of his life to have been a particular focus of lower-class hatred and discontent. One contemporary chronicler, perhaps an eye-witness, describes it:

> At last they came to the Savoy itself and broke open the gates and entered the place and came to the wardrobe and took all the torches they could find and put them in the fire; and all the cloths and coverlets and beds and hangings of great value, whereof one with heraldic shields was said to be worth a thousand marks and all the napery and other goods which they could find they carried into the hall and set fire to them with torches, and they burned the hall and chambers and all the rooms within the gates belonging to the place or manor which the London mob had left without guard. And it was said that they found three barrels of gunpowder and, thinking it was gold or silver, they threw it into the fire, and it exploded and set the hall on fire and in flame more quickly than the other did, to the great discomfort and damage of the Duke of Lancaster.[4]

Although it is fairly certain that Chaucer was in London at this time, we have no way of learning whether he and Philippa were at home in Aldgate when the infuriated, lawless crowd broke through. Those must have been very anxious days for the Chaucers. Geoffrey was by now a well-known man in London, who had long served the royal family and was closely associated with the court of Richard II and with the hated John of Gaunt. Furthermore, as comptroller of the wool custom at the port, he figured as one of the despised tax men. And if that were not enough, his wife was a Fleming, from a fairly prominent Flemish family.

Characteristically, in all of Chaucer's writing there is only one clear reference to that terrible, bloody early summer of 1381, a mild joke in the *Nun's Priest's Tale* about the racket Jack Straw's rebels had made in the streets. Unlike his friend and fellow poet John Gower, whose works contain several long, schoolmasterly lectures to the lords of the land on how to keep such crazed outlaws in their place, Chaucer never thought of his poetry as a means of social or political reform. His *Canterbury Tales,* mostly written much later, not infrequently show a warm human sympathy, or an amused roguish fascination, with individual members of the peasantry and lower classes, but he was more than likely relieved and pleased when King Richard put down the rebellion, using a characteristic mixture of great style and courage with downright bad faith at the peace parley, at which the rebel leader Wat Tyler was killed. Indeed, a man Chaucer knew from dealings in the customs house, the lord mayor of London, William Wallworth, had been the person who pulled Tyler from his horse and helped an attendant squire murder him on the ground.

It may be hard not to wish that Chaucer had raised his arm or at least his voice on the side of suffering peasants pushed beyond the limits of endurance, but we shall probably do better not to try to sanctify him just because of the wit, humanity, and great beauty of the poetry he left us. Chaucer was a man who in a very real sense lived by his wits, who rose from a comfortable middle-class family to survive unscathed a prominent thirty-year career in the complex, treacherous, sophisticated, cutthroat worlds of the royal court, international diplomacy and big-city politics. It is to be supposed that tough realism, skill, and luck had more to do with it than any amount of sweet, hopeful innocence.

The middle years of the 1380s were in some important ways a watershed in Chaucer's life. Now in his early or mid-forties, he had done important, rewarding work both for the crown and in the city. He had finished a splendid burst of poetic production that included the first of his two enduring masterpieces, *Troilus and Criseyde.* Then, in October 1385, he was appointed justice of the peace for the shire of Kent, a change that moved him out of London for a while and which also opened a new phase of political activity.

According to a slightly earlier commission of appointment for a justice of the peace, the duties were "to take surety of the peace and surety for good behavior from those who threatened bodily harm or arson. With a quorum they were to inquire by sworn inquest concerning all kinds of felonies, trespasses, forestalling, regrating, extortion, walking or riding armed in conventicles, lying in ambush to maim or kill, illegal use of liveries for maintenance, offences of hostelers who broke the laws concerning weights and measures and the sale of victuals, and offences of labourers against the labour laws."[5]

This appointment, like a few others in Chaucer's career, seems to imply some expertise in the law and its practice, whether or not he had, as some scholars have conjectured, some formal training at the Inns of Court. A statute enacted about five years before he received this commission required that the panel of justices of the peace for each county should include "un seigneur, trois ou quatre de meultz vauez du countee, [and] . . . ascuns sages de la ley"[6] (a nobleman, three or four wealthy men of the county, and some learned in the law). If the statute was being strictly enforced, Chaucer could only have qualified in the last category.

For several years he apparently lived in Kent, and his name appears in several records concerning that county, by far the most important of them being one that attests his election to Parliament in August 1386 as knight of the shire for Kent. He evidently served only one term in the House of Commons, October to November 1386, but once again it was an experience that must have tested his survival skills in the lethal game of fourteenth-century politics. For this was the Parliament in which the Commons, with Chaucer a sitting member, openly defied the king whom Chaucer had served for nearly ten years. It even impeached the royal chancellor and imposed upon Richard II a council to be chosen by Parliament. Before we applaud too hastily this apparent rising of the fourteenth-century commoners against royal tyranny, it should be noted that much of what was going on in that 1386 parliamentary session was a power struggle among the crown and the two powerful baronial houses that a century later would fight the fierce war of the Roses, Lancaster and Gloucester. Geoffrey Chaucer had long had connections of great value to him personally and professionally with both houses.

Crow and Olson, in one of the notable comic understatements of recent scholarship, remark: "His experience as a knight of the shire for Kent doubtless added to the wide and multifarious acquaintance with life which was one of his most important characteristics as a poet."[7] The fact that he survived as a knight of the shire for Kent with his head still on his shoulders and fourteen years of useful public life ahead of him attests even more to supreme mastery of the prime political skill, self-preservation.

After that stormy Parliament, Chaucer returned to Kent, where he continued to serve as justice of the peace until 1389. Then another royal appointment confirmed that he was still playing successfully the three-cornered game among burghers, barons, and throne. But during those Kentish years, probably in the summer following his term in Parliament, Philippa, his wife of more than twenty years, died. We know this because she is recorded as having been paid a regular installment of her annuity on 13 June 1387, and then on 7 November Geoffrey is paid only his own portion and there is no further trace of Philippa in the records.

There is no way of knowing what the loss of Philippa meant to him. Neither Chaucer himself nor contemporary records tell us anything about his personal or family life, and to speculate about it over the distance of six hundred years seems unprofitable, though some scholars have done so at great length. We are not sure how many children the Chaucers had, although Thomas Chaucer was nearly certainly the oldest son, and there was probably another son named Lewis, whom Geoffrey addressed as "lyte Lowys my sone" at the beginning of his *Treatise on the Astrolabe*. Much less certain is Elizabeth Chausier (in some records Chaucy), possibly Geoffrey and Philippa's daughter, for whom John of Gaunt paid some expenses when she became a nun in Barking Abbey. But it is only the name that suggests a connection with Geoffrey's family.

Thomas Chaucer, as it developed, became a wealthy landed gentleman, and had a long and distinguished career as a public servant that outshone that of his father. He, too, sat in Parliament, and was once speaker of the House of Commons; he made an excellent marriage to Maud, daughter of Sir John Burgersh; and their daughter Alice became by her marriage duchess of Suffolk. In the parish church at Ewelme, in Oxfordshire, there is still to be seen a beautiful tomb brass memorializing Thomas and Maud.

To return to the 1380s, we must at the very least consider Philippa's death one of several events near mid-decade marking major changes in Chaucer's life. He has moved away from London, left his job in the customs, become a widower, and temporarily at least removed himself from the king's service. He has put behind him the dream poems and *Troilus and Criseyde* and, as nearly as we can make out now, is to spend the rest of his life working on the grand, never-to-be-completed masterpiece of experimental poetry, the *Canterbury Tales*. But by the end of the decade Chaucer was back in the king's service, and during his remaining ten years he was usually busy in one office or another, though most of the appointments differed from those he had held in the seventies and eighties.

On 12 July 1389 Chaucer was appointed, by the same King Richard II who had been confronted and defied by the Parliament of 1386, to the important and demanding position of "Clerk of the King's Works at Westminster, the Tower of London, and other castles, manors, lodges, etc." And a year later, the administration of the remodeling of St. George's Chapel in the royal castle at Windsor was added to these responsibilities. To his previously demonstrated skills as courtier, customs officer, diplomat, shire official, and parliamentary representative, Chaucer now added those of administrative overseer of a major department of the king's household—a department with a large budget and a high visibility in the public buildings whose display value in an age which greatly valued pomp and ceremony nearly equaled their practical necessity. As Crow and Olson describe the position,

> It was an administrative post with considerable responsibilities and well defined duties, especially with respect to accounting. No evidence has been found that a technical knowledge of architecture was required, although a great builder, William of Wykeham, had before Chaucer's time been clerk of the works. As the records show, the clerk of the works arranged for the procurement, transportation and care of a great store of many kinds of building materials, tools, implements, containers, machines, etc., needed for construction and repair. If any of these materials were carried away, he had to see that they were brought back. Also, he had to supervise the sale of branches and bark from the trees purveyed for the king's works. He was not, however, responsible for the furnishings in the buildings of which he was in charge.[8]

Whatever may have been Chaucer's knowledge of architecture, builders, or architects, we again note that he found his way, as he did all through his life, to the best and most accomplished men working around him. One of the major projects completed during his tenure as clerk of the works was the rebuilding of the nave of Westminster Abbey, for which he employed Henry Yevely, one of the greatest of the late medieval architects and craftsmen in stone and especially in that most beautiful of building materials, native English oak. Tourists in the Houses of Parliament today still admire Yevely's breathtaking oak-timbered hammer-beam roof in Westminster Great Hall. Note, however, that this particular project was not undertaken by Yevely until after Chaucer left office.

As Chaucer's nineteenth-century admirers frequently remind us, his experience embraced the whole spectrum of fourteenth-century English life—and so it was for him as clerk of the works. Beside the glories of the abbey nave and the lists and grandstands for the great Smithfield tournament, the record also witnesses that in September 1390, on the road from London to the manor of Eltham (where he was in charge of the king's works), he was set upon and robbed by a gang of three or four professional thieves. In fact, the confusing court record seems to imply that the same gang mugged him again a few days later, near the appropriately named "fowle ok" (foul oak) in Hatcham, Surrey. They were caught, however, and one of them, a Richard Brierly, was hanged.

Chaucer continued as clerk of the king's works until June 1391, but even before he left that office he began to take on others. In March 1390, after a disastrous spring windstorm and flooding along the lower Thames, he was named to a commission to survey damages to walls, dikes, ditches, etc., along the river between Woolwich and Greenwich. Such commissions not only assessed damages, but also "gave orders in detail for repairs and took bonds for the performance of the repairs from the tenants, who were obliged to maintain the dykes. The commissioners also issued general orders for such measures as the planting of willows along the edges of the dykes and the ringing of pigs to protect the banks." So it looks as though some of Chaucer's experience as justice of the peace was again being called upon. It might be interesting to know what the aging diplomat, courtier, and administrator thought about tramping the wet, muddy Thames banks in the raw, windy English early spring. He may well have had a personal interest in the survey, since it covered ground in Kent near where he apparently continued to live until past the mid-1390s.

Also in 1390, Chaucer took a post that he seems to have occupied for the rest of his life, and which probably was the last of his public offices. It involved a connection with the management of the forests at Petherton Park, far to the east of London in Somersetshire and then in the possession of Roger Mortimer, earl of March. Exactly what Chaucer did in that office and how he came by it remain unknown, although he had early connections with the Mortimers. Most probably we have here an example of the widespread medieval practice of "farming" positions, with each successive "farmer" skimming part of the income. In any case, no record indicates that Chaucer ever lived in or visited North Petherton; indeed, all the indications are that he lived the last three or four years of his life in his native London.

It is amply attested that Chaucer remained in royal favor during his last years. In 1394 Richard II granted him an annuity of £20 for life "because of good service," and when, in 1399, John of Gaunt's son Henry Bolingbroke deposed Richard and took the throne as Henry IV, he promptly granted an additional 40-mark annuity "pro bono servicio quod dilectus armiger Galfridus Chaucer nobis impendit"[9] (for good service which the beloved esquire Geoffrey Chaucer has rendered). This last grant, which helped to insure that Chaucer lived comfortably to the end of his days, may have come at least partly in response to one of the last poems he wrote, the graceful and witty begging poem addressed to the new king, *The Complaint of Chaucer to his Purse*.

We do not yet have evidence of precisely when Chaucer moved back into London from Kent, but on Christmas Eve 1399, he signed a fifty-three-year lease on a dwelling in the grounds of Westminster Abbey, adjoining the garden of the Lady Chapel. It is another of those feeble seminar-room jokes that a man somewhere between fifty-five and sixty (a goodly old age by fourteenth-century standards) should sign such a long lease, but it quickly appears more sensible when we note that a few years later that lease came into the hands of his son Thomas, who held it until his own death in 1434.

On 5 June 1400, the books of the royal exchequer show that one Henry Somer paid to Geoffrey Chaucer an installment of £5 on his annuity. This is the last time Chaucer is mentioned in any public record. A century and a half later, in 1556, a stone plaque was placed over his tomb in the south transept of Westminster Abbey, recording his death date as 25 October 1400. There seems to be no reason to doubt the accuracy of the date. Let us hope that England had one of its occasional Keatsian dry sunny summers and autumns in 1400, so that the man who had written all his life beautiful poetry about formal gardens was able at the end to enjoy his lodgings in those of the abbey.

About forty-five years after the stone stating Chaucer's death date was put in place over his tomb, the poet Edmund Spenser, one of the greatest admirers and assimilators of Chaucer's poetry, requested that he be buried next to Chaucer, and so began the tradition of the "Poets' Corner." Thus Spenser helped to mark for us the real importance of Chaucer's life, the body of poetry that the public records never mention and in which Chaucer recorded nothing of the career we have been following here. It is the poetry, and the late medieval artistic and intellectual life that helped produce it, to which we shall now turn.

Chapter Two

Medieval Theories of Poetry

Near the beginning of his first major poem, the *Book of the Duchess,* Chaucer pictures himself in bed late one night reading a book of old stories:

> That clerkes had in olde tyme,
> And other poets, put in rime
> to rede, and for to be in minde
> While men loved the law of kinde.
> (53–56)[1]

A few lines further along, he says that one of the sad stories affected him so deeply

> That trewely I, which made this book,
> Had such pitee and such rowthe
> To rede hir sorwe, that, by my trowthe,
> I ferde the worse al the morwe
> Aftir, to thenken on hir sorwe.
> (96–100)

These lines were written early in his career, but he felt secure enough in his poetic identity to undertake the formidably delicate task of composing a consolatory elegy for the great duke of Lancaster on the death of his wife. The ideas they express about why poetry is made and what it does reflect for us with instructive accuracy a traditional academic poetic orthodoxy that obviously helped to shape the young poet's sense of his craft.

To convert Chaucer's personal immediacy to impersonal text-book abstraction, these lines tell us that it is the purpose of poetry to preserve the wisdom of the past ("That clerkes had in olde tyme, / and other poets, put in rime") and the truth of nature ("the law of kinde"); and that both writer and reader are motivated to this engagement with truth and sustained in it by strong emotions ("While men *loved* the lawe of kinde"; "I, which made this book, / Had such pitee and such rowthe . . .").

This sense of central balance—and often tension—between knowledge and feeling, intellect and emotion, goes back as far as the earliest records we have of men's efforts to analyze and justify the uses of persuasive language, of language that seeks to convince by arousing or pleasing its audience. Plato had concluded that all attempts to manipulate emotion through language were unjustifiable, so he banned both rhetoricians and poets from his ideal republic. Aristotle subsequently set about rehabilitating both, in his well-known treatises on rhetoric and poetics, on the grounds that emotive uses of language were fundamentally human and necessary.[2] From Cicero in the first century B.C. through the Sophist rhetoricians of the first and second centuries A.D., we can follow a running debate over the relative efficacy (and moral defensibility) of reason and emotion in persuasive discourse. The Roman poet Horace, a younger contemporary of Cicero's, based his famous and influential theory of poetry in the *Epistle to the Pisos* on a precise balance of the two, formulated in the phrase that was to be echoed for centuries after his time, "dulce et utile" (literally, the sweet and the useful). Chaucer reflects the phrase in a marvellously witty pastiche of warped paraphrase from Horace at the opening of his *Parliament of Fowls*:

> Of usage—what for lust and what for lore—
> On bokes rede I ofte, as I yow tolde.
> But wherefore that I speke al this? Nat yoore
> Agon it happede me for to beholde
> Upon a bok, was write with lettres olde,
> And thereupon, a certeyn thing to lerne,
> The longe day ful faste I redde and yerne.
> (15–21)

Although the classical and medieval terms of the argument may seem remote from us, the issue itself should not. It is still very much alive today, underlying both the Marxist critics' demand for instructive social realism in art and the sophisticated aesthete's moral indignation over Madison Avenue hucksterism. We need also to remember that it was centuries after Chaucer's time before anyone ventured to argue openly that beauty was its own justification or to articulate a theory of art based on the premise that play and pleasure are so necessarily human that they need no other defense. As H. L. Mencken told us acerbly in his essay on our American Puritan heritage,[3] many of us still carry in our veins a troublesome strain of the blood of our pilgrim forefathers, which makes us uneasy, guilty, or angry in the presence of any pleasure to which we cannot assign an ulterior moral or (preferably) financial purpose.

Although there had been many people during the centuries between Horace and Chaucer who maintained, like Plato, that artistic creation was either bad in itself or at best playing with fire, creating temptations that incurred risks too great for sinful man to bear, Chaucer unmistakably believed in his poetic craft and its usefulness to others as well as in its challenges and rewards to himself. But the writers who had nourished that belief for him and helped him define it as well as explore its limitations, were not mainly the great Greeks and Romans mentioned above, although he had some knowledge of them, most of it indirect. Rather, it was the medieval Christian writers he knew best, starting with Augustine and Boethius. Their work, although it descends directly from the classical theorists of rhetoric, places the issue in a context of very different theories of knowledge and values.

The most recent historian of medieval rhetoric, which in this period we may take to include nearly all thinking and theorizing about language and its uses, says of the situation in which Augustine found himself at the end of the fourth century:

> The basic issue was whether the church should adopt completely the contemporary culture which Rome had taken over from Greece. The fate of rhetoric, as a part of Greco-Roman culture, was involved not only in the debate over the larger issue but in more limited controversies about its own merits. Indeed, the contrast between *Verbum* (Word of God) and *verbum* (word of man) was stressed from the very beginnings of the Church, long before the broader cultural issue was joined.
>
> Ecclesiastical leaders of the fourth century continued the debate begun more than a century earlier when the conversion of many writers, poets, orators, and public figures had at last given the Church a corps of well equipped apologists.[4]

Augustine had himself been trained in the Roman schools of rhetoric and, on the evidence of his own writings, was widely and deeply read in classical poetry and drama, the pleasures of which he never completely rejected, unlike his friend and contemporary Jerome. On the contrary, his gift to the later Middle Ages was a prototypical formulation of a defensible Christian art of discourse deliberately willing to risk the pleasingly attractive embodiment of truths that fallen and willful men might otherwise never learn. He was even able to recommend to at least some of his fellow Christians the study of great secular writers—even pagan ones—in order to learn and reuse their stylistic devices.

It is true that Augustine nowhere specifically extends his notion of a Christian art of discourse to include poetry; the ideas we are most concerned with here are expressed most fully in the fourth book of *De doctrina Christiana,* a work in which he was clearly writing for the benefit of Christian preachers. However, the characteristically Augustinian uneasy balancing of truth and delight has in it much of the concern for the *dulce et utile* that Horace had found distinctive of good poetry. And subsequent medieval theorists do stretch persuasive rhetoric to include poetry,[5] offering for it the same defenses Augustine had offered for artful preaching.

At the opening of chapter 2 of book 4 of *De doctrina Christiana*, Augustine articulates that defense firmly and clearly:

> Since persuasion both to truths and falsehoods is urged by means of the art of rhetoric, who would venture to say that truth, in the person of its defenders, ought to stand its ground, unarmed, against falsehood, so that those who are trying to convince us of falsehoods should know how to induce their listeners to be favorably inclined, attentive, and docile . . . while the defenders of truth do not know how to do this? . . . The power of eloquence—so very effective in convincing us of either wrong or right—lies open to all. Why then, do not the good zealously procure it that it may serve truth, if the wicked, in order to gain unjustifiable and groundless cases, apply it to the advantages of injustice and error?[6]

In the centuries following Augustine, as the increasingly institutionalized Christian church became an educational institution as well, these central Augustinian issues remained fundamental and often hotly controversial among Christian intellectuals, although often in much mutated forms. Then, too, by the time we reach the golden age of the medieval universities—the twelfth and thirteenth centuries—the issues have acquired a new dimension. By then, it was not only a question of learning from pagans (or rationally inventing) emotional techniques to lead men to God, but also of recovering a now almost unimaginably remote past and the things worth preserving from it. Much of what we know and much of what Chaucer knew of late medieval theories of literature comes from textbooks written for university courses designed to preserve viable knowledge of the Latin language and the great body of human thought preserved in it.

Thus, much more slowly and circuitously than this brief condensation implies, but unmistakably nevertheless, orthodox academic theorists of the twelfth and thirteenth centuries had come to attribute to the language of poetry not only the Augustinian commitments to technical persuasive skill and the right moral purpose, but a historical commitment as well. Good literature not only instructed through delight, but also preserved the past. And perhaps we need to remind ourselves that for the Middle Ages, the past meant almost exclusively the literary past—what was recorded in books. No archaeology, no paleoanthropology, no carbon-14 readings, only the penetration and interpretation of the languages of other men and other times.

The result is that there are two constants in the late twelfth- and early thirteenth-century textbooks for the university courses in *rhetorica*, courses that presumed to teach not only how to interpret great Latin poetry of the past, but how to write its modern equivalent. First, they all insist on an elaborate and, to us, often bizarrely arbitrary attention to the mechanics of style, including metaphor, simile, and word patterns like repetition and puns. Second, they all assume that the writer will be working from a traditional model, either a specific work that is being "translated,"[7] or a theme time-tested and given a traditional shape in the accumulated literature of the past.

A near contemporary of Chaucer's, from whom Chaucer took more for his own use than from any other writer except the Roman Ovid, sums up very precisely the ideas I have just been outlining. Boccaccio, in the introduction to his *De genealogia deorum*, writes:

> Some men have thought that the learned poet merely invents shallow tales, and is therefore not only useless, but a positive harm. This is because they read discursively and, of course, derive no profit from the story. Now this work of mine removes the veil from these inventions, shows that poets were really men of wisdom, and renders their compositions full of profit and pleasure to the reader. So, if poets who seemed to have perished from want of appreciation are now brought back to life, as it were, and to a high place in the state, while their usefulness to the individual, which was ignored because it was unrecognized, is now revealed by this work of mine, they thus rouse the reader's mind to higher feelings. Furthermore, I hope that men will rise up as they have done in the past who will devote themselves to the study of poetry. As they peruse the memorials and remains of the Ancients, they cannot fail to derive much help from this work of mine, which will prove valuable to them if not to others.[8]

Boccaccio's absorption with the classical past has sometimes been exaggerated into a new, Renaissance humanistic break with the medieval past he reflects and continues. That, however, is an argument we need not get into here, though the focus upon Latin (and, for Boccaccio, a burgeoning new interest in Greek) remains a matter of concern, mainly because it continues to be the almost exclusive concern of medieval academic theorists. To oversimplify the matter again, what use could a writer who wanted to write a French, Italian, or English poem make of all these instructions for interpreting and rewriting Latin poems? Boccaccio, who wrote some of medieval Europe's loveliest and most lasting literature in his vernacular Italian, has nothing to say on that question, though he must have thought long and hard about it.

There is probably no medieval writer who expresses more concern in his own works for the masterful use of the vernacular (in his case, English) than Chaucer, but only two theoretical essays devoted to that specific subject survive, neither by him. Both are by writers whose work he knew thoroughly, Dante Alighieri and Eustace Deschamps, but there is no specific indication in his writing that he was acquainted with either Dante's *De vulgari eloquentia* or Deschamps's *L'art de dictier et de fere chancons*. Both of these treatises deal with issues that Chaucer expressed concern about throughout his writing career; both draw heavily on the academic tradition we have been discussing, which Chaucer knew thoroughly; and the real differences between the two tell us something fundamentally important about the unresolved conflict over basic issues that characterized the fourteenth-century heritage out of which Chaucer had to form his notion of what he was doing as a poet.

Dante's treatise on eloquence (by which we take him to mean, just as Augustine had meant, artful persuasion) in the vernacular is incomplete, but it is still the most extensive and penetrating early consideration of how to do in another language what the university rhetoric masters had been describing and prescribing for Latin poetry.[9] In its second book, Dante makes a simultaneous identification and distinction: "poetry . . . is nothing else but a rhetorical composition set to music." That is, he agrees with the school tradition descended from Augustine and the Roman rhetoricians that poetry has to persuade people emotionally to some desirable end, but he also wants to enphasize the importance of the "music" of language in that persuasion. Beautiful language, as poets have always known, works on us far beyond its grammatical or logical structure or its thematic referentiality. That is particularly important to Dante because he knows that although he can sing great songs in Italian, their "music" cannot ever sound the same as that of his great Latin master, Vergil. Dante's Italian was still close enough to Latin that he could write lines in the *Commedia* that are readable as either, yet he was concerned about the problem; and how much more concerned the English Chaucer must have been.

Dante perceived that in many matters—in fact, in all the basic moral, historical, and structural commitments of poetry—he should follow what he calls the "regular poets," those who wrote by the rules of the school tradition, but as the bulk of *De vulgari* emphasizes, what concerns him most is the new music, the readjustment of the old Latin stylistic apparatus that must be made by vernacular poets. That concern leads him to a fascinating analysis of metrical and prosodic structures in the vernacular lyrics, a genre none of the school texts had ever taken up, despite the fact that for two centuries before Dante's time some of Europe's most lasting and beautiful poetry was being written by lyric poets of southern France.

A generation after Dante, a contemporary and admirer of Geoffrey Chaucer, the northern French lyric poet Eustache Deschamps, wrote the second of the two surviving medieval attempts at a theory of vernacular poetry, *L'Art de dictier et de fere chancons* (The art of composing and making songs [i.e., lyric poems]). There is no way for us to know whether Deschamps knew Dante's *De vulgari eloquentia*, but like Dante he concentrates exclusively on the forms, meters, and styles of the vernacular lyric, in this case Northern French. And again like Dante, Deschamps concentrates on the music of the lyric as the essence of its art.[10] In fact, Deschamps classifies poetry as a branch of the art of music, one of the traditional seven liberal arts that formed the basis of the medieval university curriculum.

Deschamps expresses little of Dante's passionate conviction that it is the linguistic music that makes poetry the eloquent persuader he wanted it to be. Indeed, Deschamps offers no direct moral defense of poetry at all. Rather, he says "Its delectable and pleasant songs medicine and recreate those who are fatigued, heavy, or bored by thought, imagination, or labor"[11] in order that they can return refreshed to the pursuit of the other liberal arts. Perhaps the most distinctive quality of Deschamps's view of poetry is an acceptance of its purely recreational value, a nearly completely aesthetic justification.

Deschamps may have assumed that the heavy historical and moral obligations laid upon it by Dante and the school theorists belonged to another kind of writing than what he was talking about. Yet I think it is important for us to see that Deschamps's emphasis upon poetry's refreshment of the soul, heretical though it may at first appear, is not so much a radical departure from the traditional ideas as it is a sharp shift of emphasis. The *dulce*, the sweet, the delightful, had always been there in the formulations, though from Augustine on, serious defenders of literary art had to come down hard on the *utile*, the useful, moral ends of poetry, in order to defend it against those puritans who, throughout the ages, would argue that anything beautiful is too much of a temptation for sinful humanity. Fortunately, we have Deschamps to remind us that not all civilized and intelligent medieval people, however Christian, were so fearful and distrustful of the beauties of poetic artifice.

We know little about the relationship between Chaucer and Deschamps. Through the first half of his writing career, Chaucer borrowed much from Deschamps and Deschamps wrote a charming *ballade* praising Chaucer's poetry. It is evident throughout his work, especially in the early poems, that Chaucer agreed completely with Deschamps about the necessity for the *dulce* in poetry, just as he also tells us repeatedly that he shared the commitment of Dante and the university theorists to use that music in the service of worthy moral purposes.

From the Roman Ovid to the French contemporaries Machaut, Froissart, and Deschamps, the writers Chaucer admired and borrowed from most and whose art he most studied and imitated were all careful, elaborate, "artificial" managers of language, whether their language was Latin, Italian, or French. (Chaucer thought very little of most of his English contemporaries and predecessors and nearly never mentioned or emulated them.)

When he comments about stylistic techniques—as he does frequently throughout his writings—his language regularly echoes the twelfth- and thirteenth-century school treatises on the art of *elocutio*, the elaborate, artificial, verbal decoration of a theme. Two examples from the *Canterbury Tales* will illustrate the point and introduce some basic terms and ideas.

The Squire, about to describe a particularly beautiful woman, says near the beginning of his tale: "It moste been a rethor excellent, / That koude his colours longynge for that art, / If he sholde hire discryven every part" (V:38–40). And the Host, urging the Clerk of Oxford to speak simply for the common people, admonishes him: "Your termes, youre colours, and youre figures / Keepe hem in stoor til so be that ye endite / Heigh style, as whan that men to kynges write" (IV:16–18).

It is true that there is in these passages an undercurrent of good-natured irony, partly because the characters speaking are slightly pretentious and definitely not literary men; but even so they reveal a good deal about what people of Chaucer's time expected of a literary style. The same terms and expectations are used when Chaucer is speaking most seriously about his art, as he does in this famous passage from *Troilus and Criseyde*:

> But soth is, though I kan nat tellen al,
> As kan myn auctour, of his excellence,
> Yet have I seyd, and God toforn and shal
> In every thyng, al holy his sentence;
> And if that ich, at loves reverence,
> Have any word in eched for the beste,
> Doth therwithal right as yourselven leste.
>
> For myne wordes, heere and every part
> I speke hem alle under correccioun
> Of yow that felying han in loves art,
> And putte it al in youre discrecioun
> To encresse or maken dymynucioun
> Of my langage, and that I yow biseche.
> (III:1324–36)

These two stanzas come near the middle of the poem, just before a passage that Chaucer knows will put his skill to its severest test: the depiction of the consumation of Troilus and Criseyde's love, with all its human and moral significance. He begins by reminding us that he is retelling the story from an ancient source and thus placing himself in the long tradition of "auctours," so that we must judge his skill in comparison with theirs. Then, too, it is the "sentence," the core of meaning and value, that he is particularly concerned to preserve, while reclothing it in his own language. And notice how he expresses it: he is, with deliberate care and skill, "edging in" (or adding in) his own words, laying on some language of his own that was not in his "auctour," and that may be even better ("for the beste").

Notice also the last three lines of the second stanza. "Encresse" and "dymynucioun" are exact translations of the two Latin terms *amplificatio* and *abbreviatio*, which denote the two fundamental processes in the management of style as defined in the school "rhetorike" that the Squire and the Host seem to have known a bit about. *Abbreviatio* was the process of reducing your source to the material you wanted to write about; *amplificatio*, the way to make it effective by working in figures of speech ("coloures, figures, and termes") and other verbal decoration, making it in the end (at least stylistically) your own poem.

But we should return to "myn auctour" in the second line of the passage quoted, Chaucer's acknowledgment that poetry must also recover, preserve, and revivify the past. Chaucer seems to have had an especially strong sense of how the past keeps slipping away from us, constantly receding into the ever-dimming and distorting mirror of other and older languages. He frequently remarks upon his obligation, as a writer, to preserve the past and bring alive again in his own language its people and its lore, its wisdom and its follies. In the introduction to an early poem, *Anelida and Arcite*, where he is trying to remake an earlier Italian poem that Boccaccio had remade from a classical Latin poem, Chaucer wrote:

> For hit ful depe is sonken in my mynde
> With pitous hert in Englyssh to endyte
> This olde storie, in Latin which I fynde,
> Of quene Anelida and fals Arcite,
> That elde, which that al can frete and bite
> As hit hath freten many a noble storie
> Hath nygh devoured out of oure memorie.
> (8–14)

Sometimes he seems far ahead of his times in his sense of how language change affects our perception of old books and of the special burden the instability of language places on a serious writer. He puts it nicely at the beginning of the second book of *Troilus and Criseyde*, where he is especially concerned about puzzling out from his ancient sources the meaning and feeling of his great love story:

> Ye knowe ek that in forme of speche is chaunge
> Withinne a thousand yeer, and wordes tho
> That hadden pris, now wonder nyce and straunge
> Us thinketh hem, and yet they spak hem so,

And spedde as wel in love as men now do;
Ek for to wynnen love in sondry ages,
In sondry londes, sondry ben usages.
(II:22–28)

At the end of the poem, he seems almost to forsee prophetically what will happen to the English language between his time and ours—to picture us down here in the twentieth century struggling to reconstruct and understand his fourteenth-century English:

And for ther is so gret diversity
In Englissh and in writyng of our tonge,
So prey I God that non myswrite the,
Ne the mysmetre for defaute of tonge.
And red whereso thow be, or elles songe,
That thow be understonde, God I biseche.
(V:1793–99)

We see here that Chaucer, as acutely as any of the theorists who made up the tradition linking him with Augustine and the late Roman rhetoricians, knew that man was fallen and that the languages in which men's pilgrimage through time was recorded shared all the limiting mortal consequences of that fall. Like Dante and Deschamps, Chaucer knew that not only as abstract dogma, but as a primary fact in his experience of the redeeming beauty of the artful language of poetry, both other writers' and his own.

Chapter Three

The Continental Background: Chaucer's Literary Sources and Influences

The question of how other writers' work has affected the production of a particular writer and his sense of the nature and value of accumulated literary tradition is probably the most difficult issue that literary historians and critics have to face. One writer may borrow heavily from a readily identifiable source, but reshape the material so completely that the stylistic quality of the resultant work has nearly nothing in common with the source. Another writer may be profoundly influenced by the style or thematic values of an admired predecessor, yet we may scarcely be able to trace a single line or phrase to a specific model. One writer, like Walt Whitman in mid-nineteenth century America, may attempt for himself and urge upon others a complete break with the literary past in order to create a wholly new, original poetry. Others, like T. S. Eliot a couple of generations later, may complain despairingly about the impossibility of writing good poetry without a solidly established tradition to rely upon.

Such questions are germane to the study of Chaucer's work, both in the sense that its relations with that of other poets help us understand how his was made and how it functions, and in the sense that all through his poems he comments frequently about such matters, perhaps nowhere more gracefully and directly than in the "G" Prologue to the *Legend of Good Women*:

> Thanne mote we to bokes that we fynde,
> Thourgh whiche that olde thynges ben in mynde,
> And to the doctryne of these olde wyse
> Yeven credence, in every skylful wyse. . . .
> (17–20)

> For wel I wot that folk han here-beforn
> Of makyng ropen and lad awey the corn;
> And I come after, glenynge here and there,
> And am ful glad if I may fynde an ere
> Of any goodly word that they han left.
>
> (61–65)

It is fair to say that one of the major themes in Chaucer's poetry is his relationship to other poets, both ancient and modern.

Although he sometimes alludes directly to the school textbooks mentioned in the preceding chapter and to the technical ideas contained in them, most often he writes of his problems and pleasures as a poet in connection with his sense of the literary tradition in general or of individual great writers in it. An intimidatingly large amount of research during the two hundred years or so of what we might call "modern Chaucer scholarship" has been devoted to discovering exactly what Chaucer had read, identifying his literary allusions, and recovering and publishing the appropriate texts. The results have been enormously useful and so detailed and extensive, not to mention controversial, that it is impossible for an introductory volume to attempt a careful survey. Rather, I propose to indicate the general shape of Chaucer's literary indebtedness and some of the main historical and critical questions raised by his differing responses to the three main currents of literary tradition as he perceived it; Latin, French, and Italian. Inevitably, both before and after he encountered whatever he knew of the formal academic analyses of literary theory and practice, Chaucer's notions of what poetry is and how it may be made have to have been nurtured mainly by what he read and liked or disliked in the work of his contempories and predecessors.

We should probably begin with a little attention to what is *not* there in Chaucer's awareness of the usable literary tradition. For a writer so quintessentially English as Chaucer, whom perhaps only Shakespeare equaled at making high art out of a perfect ear for the beautiful basics of spoken English, it seems almost incredible that he seems largely unacquainted with and uninterested in the English poetry of his own time and the preceding century and a half.[1] When he does have something to say about any English literature, he either gives it a hilarious send-up, as in the Tale of Sir Thopas in the *Canterbury Tales*, or indirectly disparages it, as (again in the *Canterbury*

Tales) in the Parson's blunt dismissal of the best being produced by any of Chaucer's contemporaries, "I kan nat geste, rim ram ruf by lettre."

It seems hard to believe that Chaucer could so easily have dismissed the poetic accomplishment—nearly equal to his own—of *Sir Gawain and the Green Knight, Pearl,* or *Piers Plowman*. Perhaps he really did not know of them, or, as has been argued, their West Midland dialects of Middle English were too different from his own native London dialect to afford him a real appreciation of the stylistic beauties of their alliterative verse, although he seems to have had no trouble with the equally different Northern dialect and even had a good deal of fun reproducing some of it in the Reeve's Tale.

Whatever the precise historical details, it will help if we can see—as Dante had argued in *De vulgari eloquentia*—that the raw materials fed into a poet's imagination are distilled finally into his own filed, fitted, and polished version of his own language, his particular vernacular music. If Chaucer did not think much of what his compatriots had written in English, that does not mean that he lacked a compelling sense of what might be done with it.

Another block of medieval Europe's best poetry that seems to have been outside Chaucer's knowledge was the rich and diverse Middle High German poetry of the twelfth, thirteenth, and fourteenth centuries, the *Nibelungenlied*, the lyrics of the minnesingers, and Arthurian romances such as Wolfram's *Parzifal*. Chaucer had probably never encountered them. His foreign travels seem never to have taken him to any German-speaking states, and it is likely that his linguistic versatility did not extend to Middle High German.

Similarly, he seems to have been largely unacquainted with the literature of medieval Spain, although it has become clear recently that he accompanied Edward the Black Prince on a brief excursion into northern Spain. It is thought possible that he was aware of the medieval Spanish poem *La celestina*, which may have contributed to the creation of the Wife of Bath's character in the *Canterbury Tales*.

We return then to the three large literatures that Chaucer grew up with, which throughout his life as a writer were his primary instructors in what poetry is and the providers of much of the material out of which he made it. This triad—Latin, French, and Italian—should be seen also as a rough chronological succession of cultural dominance. The first, classical Latin, meant to the Middle Ages mainly the Roman writers of the first century B.C. and on through to the fall of Rome in the fifth century A.D., the same Latin classics that provided the basis for most academic study of literature until well into the nineteenth century.

A second Latin literature of importance to Chaucer and other medieval writers was the vast and varied accumulation of postclassical, Christian, medieval writing in Latin. Nearly all the serious intellectual discourse of Europe, from the fifth century well into the sixteenth, was conducted in Latin. This included a good deal of poetry, as well as scientific and philosophical treatises, doctrinal expositions, school textbooks, saints' lives, histories, and occasional cabbages and kings.

But in more strictly and conventionally literary terms, the twelfth and thirteenth centuries saw the emergence of an exciting new poetry in France—first in the lyrics of the south (Provence) and then in the longer narrative and allegorical poems of the north—that quickly became the dominant influence throughout European vernacular poetry. From then on, although the classical Roman poets continued to be studied and admired and occasionally imitated (as they still are), poetry written in Latin and closely based on Latin models steadily declined.

Then, well into the thirteenth century, Italian poets—like their German, English, and Spanish colleagues—began to develop the lessons they had learned from their French exemplars into a distinctive vernacular poetry all their own. By the end of the century, one of the giants of medieval vernacular poetry, Dante Alighieri, brought this flowering to an incomparable fruition, first in his *Vita nuova* and then in the *Divine Comedy*. In the next generation Giovanni Boccaccio and Francesco Petracco (Petrarch) added their very differently compelling accomplishments to Dante's to provide the foundation of an Italian dominance of European literature for the next two centuries. That dominance, together with a comparable flowering of the other arts and sciences, is what we have since learned to call the Italian Renaissance.

Geoffrey Chaucer of late fourteenth-century London was singularly fortunate to have been born in a time when he could easily learn, respond to, and reuse as his own all three of these great literary cultures. The Latin tradition, both classical and medieval, was declining, but still very much alive, and though Chaucer was not a schoolman, it is obvious that he was more familiar with that literature and comfortable with it than most of us will ever be. The masterpiece of thirteenth-century French, *Le roman de la rose,* was a century old in Chaucer's day, already a "classic" and so important to the naturally bilingual Chaucer that he made his own English translation. And—this is especially important—a new group of young French poets, Chaucer's contemporaries Machaut, Froissart, and Deschamps, was creating a "new wave" of poetry derived from their thirteenth-century masters. Chaucer, always in touch with the avant-garde of his age, knew their work from his youth and probably knew them, at least Deschamps, personally as well. Finally, two or three generations before other English writers had begun to take any significant interest in their work, Chaucer had familiarized himself with the writings of the three giants of Italian poetry, Dante, Boccaccio, and Petrarch.

Let us begin with the Roman classics. Chaucer's knowledge of them has been much studied. There is no need to list all the classical authors he is thought to have read, read parts of, or heard of in other people's work. Two of them, Ovid and Vergil (perhaps a third, Statius), were unarguably of major importance to him. Beyond those three (we are talking now only about the pre-Christian, classical Roman writers), it is hard to pin down just what Chaucer knew first-hand and what he knew at second or third hand. As observed in the preceding chapter, medieval writers, even as early as Augustine, were concerned with preserving and representing what they could salvage from their classical past. All sorts of collections of favorite quotations, summaries of important works, digests of famous texts and commentaries on them, thumbnail biographies and ready-reference handbooks were in existence to preserve and pass on a kind of knowledge of classical authors that large numbers of their compilers and readers could certainly never have known completely. Thousands of people in the English-speaking world today know Shakespeare, for instance, in somewhat the same way, never having seen or read his plays and possibly not able to date his life accurately within two or three centuries, but still they are perfectly assured that he was "a great," that he had something to do with Hamlet and Romeo and Juliet, and that he said profound things like "lay on, Macduff," "to be or not to be," and "a rose by any other name would smell as sweet." That may sound too condescending, but surely Chaucer and many other medieval readers knew much of the classical past in something like that way. It is a matter we shall return to, but for Ovid and Vergil at least, there is solid ground to stand on.

Almost from his own time, Vergil was nearly universally considered the standard of poetic excellence, the master all should emulate, but would probably never equal. Some puritanical medieval churchmen thought such powerful writing by a pagan very dangerous (one thirteenth-century cleric called the *Aeneid* "a beautiful vase full of vipers"), but the schools regularly used Vergil as a model both for Latin language and for poetic style. Students were asked to translate passages from the *Aeneid* and then, laying the original aside, put their translations back into Latin poetry, which the masters would then judge against the original. It is doubtful that Chaucer had that sort of rigorous formal schooling in Vergil, but it is evident from his poetry that he knew the *Aeneid* thoroughly. He probable did not, however, know Vergil's *Eclogues* or *Georgics.* Recent scholarship has discovered that Chaucer made use of a partial summary and commentary on the *Aeneid,* called *Ilias,* by a French cleric, Simon Aurea Capra. In fact, rather frequently when Chaucer uses a Latin source, he finds another version or redaction or commentary to use along with it, so that his reading of the *Aeneid*, for instance, was probably much affected by the readings of other medieval commentators.

Almost the only direct borrowing from the *Aeneid* by Chaucer comes in the first book of the *House of Fame,* where he retells at some length the story of Aeneas' love affair with Dido in Carthage. It is a curious passage and there has been much puzzled disagreement among critics about it. Chaucer completely alters the tone, psychology, and moral thrust of Vergil's version, converting the epic into a typically medieval account of a beautiful noble lady "falsed" in love, a common type of medieval fiction we now call "romance."

Chaucer speaks frequently of Vergil, always with the greatest respect and admiration, but there is nothing in Chaucer's poetry that anyone would rightly call Vergilian, not even that one extended passage from the *Aeneid.* Whatever it was that attracted him to the *Aeneid*, whatever effect Vergil had on Chaucer's ideas of poetic style and purpose, by the time it was distilled into his own personal, witty, ironic, often comic style, it had become impossible for the reader to recognize.

With Ovid, the case is different. From his first major poem, the *Book of the Duchess,* to his last great work, the *Canterbury Tales,* bits and pieces of Ovidian material are scattered all through Chaucer's poems. Also, increasingly in the past two or three decades, critics have felt a genuine affinity between Chaucer's tone and style and those of the elegant, urbane, witty, and sometimes cynical Ovid. Indeed, John Dryden, the first critic to write extensively about the *Canterbury Tales,* in the preface to his *Fables* late in the seventeenth century, began with a perceptive and still convincing comparison of Chaucer with Ovid. It is true that Chaucer is frequently sentimental where Ovid is cynical, his irony less brittle and cutting than Ovid's. And Chaucer's versions of sexual relations can be at times very romantically idealized, while Ovid's are usually at least coolly objective, sometimes cynically dirty-minded.

Some of these differences can be accounted for by the fact that Chaucer seems to have liked best and used most Ovid's *Metamorphoses.* While many modern classicists would probably consider the *Remedia amoris* more typical of Ovid's work (and Chaucer probably knew the *Remedia*), it was the softer and less ironic *Metamorphoses* that Chaucer quarried for story materials. The opening story of Ceyx and Alcione in the *Book of the Duchess* comes from it and so do most of the stories retold in the *Legend of Good Women* and the basic stories of some of the *Canterbury Tales.*

Again, we must take into account the large body of medieval Christian commentary that had accumulated around Ovid, just as it had around Vergil. And much more than with Vergil, medieval Christian intellectuals found it necessary to justify reading the frank, sophisticated pagan Ovid by constructing elaborate semiallegorical ethical and moral "interpretations" of his work. Typical of this strange and strained medieval procedure is the French *Ovide Moralisé,* a thirteenth-century conversion of the *Metamorphoses* into a collection of Christian moral lessons. It is hard to say to what extent such exegetical materials blurred Chaucer's perception of Ovid's true tone and attitudes, but at least some of the time he must simply have read and delighted in the old Roman's work, despite the overlays of earnest Christian glossing.

There are several other classical writers—Cicero, Horace, and Seneca, for instance—with whose names and reputations, at least, Chaucer probably had some acquaintance. But there is only one other whose work we must consider here, because it provided substance of major importance to Chaucer. In the first century A.D., Statius wrote his long epic about the siege of Thebes, the *Thebaid.* It remained fairly popular throughout the Middle Ages, partly because, like Vergil's *Aeneid* and several other classical works, it was considered to be also a kind of history, a preservation of factual knowledge about the otherwise irrecoverable past.

Over a period of at least twenty years, Chaucer made two—perhaps three—attempts to reduce the scale of the *Thebiad*, choosing parts that interested him most and remaking them somewhat as he had remade the Dido and Aeneas episode from Vergil's *Aeneid*.[2] And here too, as with Vergil and Ovid, Chaucer used an intermediary source that did much to direct his response to Statius. Earlier in the fourteenth century Boccaccio, partly translating Statius but using other sources as well, had written a long epic in Italian, the *Teseida*. (The title is not a translation of *Thebaid,* but rather a similar epic title derived from the name of Theseus, the king who commanded the siege of Thebes.)

Early in his career—the dating of Chaucer's poems is always partly guesswork—he made an abortive first attempt, lifting out the love story of Queen Anelida and the knight Arcite, another one of those tales of "falsed" ladies, and turning it into perhaps the most metrically and stylistically complicated thing he ever wrote, but one that he broke off after 357 lines, nearly as soon as the story had started. Then, in the Prologue to his *Legend of Good Women*, probably written about 1386, he mentions among his earlier works a poem about "al the love of Palamon and Arcite," another piece surely derived from *Thebaid/Teseida*. There is no extant text of this work, but the first and longest, and one of the most impressive of the *Canterbury Tales* is the Knight's tale of Palamon and Arcite, in which Chaucer succeeds notably in reducing the epic of the siege of Thebes to a medieval romance about the conflict of two young knights for the love of the beautiful Emily, daughter of Theseus.

The other Latin tradition, the medieval Christian one stretching from Augustine and Boethius down to Chaucer, is far longer, more varied, and thinner in material of primarily literary merit than the two or three centuries of Roman writing we have just considered. It is consequently much harder to simplify into some pattern appropriate to the kind of introduction I wish to provide. A major reason for that is that much, perhaps most, of what Chaucer took from the later Latin writers was information rather than stories or models of style and structure. The great bulk, though certainly not all, of that medieval Latin literature was doctrinal, philosophical, scientific, historical, and pedagogical. These are all areas in which Chaucer shows a continuing interest and in which he had read suprisingly widely for a secular man whose professional career was that of politician and public servant. But most of what comes through in his poetry from that wide reading is specific allusion to particular bits of knowledge or interpretation.

One enormous exception to my last generalization is the late fifth-early sixth-century Roman Christian, Boethius, whose *De consolatione philosophiae,* written while he was in prison awaiting death on a charge of treason, profoundly affected nearly all later medieval Christian thought. Chaucer's poems, from earliest to last, are full of echoes of Boethian language, reflections of Boethian ideas about fortune, mortality, and material and spiritual goods. Also, somewhere near the middle of his career,[3] Chaucer made a complete translation into Middle English of the *De consolatione.* The *Book of the Duchess, Troilus and Criseyde,* the Knight's tale—none of these could have been what they are without the Boethian borrowings Chaucer wove into them.

There are a few other exceptions, too, though none as strikingly important as Boethius. The long Christian allegorical poem *De planctu naturae* (The complaint of nature), by the twelfth-century monk Alanus de Insulis, a typically medieval interfusion of science, theology, and moral philosphy, provided Chaucer with material for an important part of the *Parliament of Fowls.* And a long opening section of the same poem—a passage almost as puzzling to modern critics as the Dido and Aeneas passage in the *House of Fame*—is based on another widely popular medieval work, Macrobius's edition (with a long interpretative commentary) of Cicero's *Somnium Scipionis* (Scipio's dream), a work probably put together about 400 A.D. In addition, for several of the saints' lives in the *Canterbury Tales,* as well as for allusions elsewhere in his work, Chaucer relies on Jacobus de Voragine's thirteenth-century collection of saints' lives, the *Legenda aurea* (Golden legend). Some critics have suggested that the *Legend of Good Women,* also titled the *Saints' Legend of Cupid,* may have been Chaucer's deliberate artistic inversion of the framing idea of the *Legenda aurea.* Finally, we should probably mention a considerable body of scientific writing on astronomy and astrology, in which Chaucer maintained a lifelong interest. In 1391, he wrote—apparently for his son Lewis—a *Treatise on the Astrolabe* (an instrument used in astronomic calculations), in which he made use of a variety of such sources.

In considering Chaucer's French sources, we face a problem similar to that of the Latin tradition. He was widely read in the French literature of the thirteenth and fourteenth centuries,[4] and it provides him not only with a constant source of generic models, themes, ideas, and story matter, but also with his primary sense of stylistic artifice and the basic music of his versification. So very basic is this late medieval French literature to Chaucer's notion of what it means to write poetry that, early in this century, an eminent French medievalist was willing to argue that we really ought to consider Chaucer a French poet who just happened to write in English.[5] But as many English readers quickly protested, Chaucer always conveys a quality of profound Englishness. Yet we can understand how the French scholar, shrewdly assessing the matrix of poetic notions medieval French poetry had provided him, could have come to think such a thing.

In the next chapter, we will consider the development of Chaucer's prosody out of the French tradition. Our main business in this chapter is to report the overall shape of his responses to French literature. Somewhat arbitrarily, but I think usefully, we may begin by splitting the subject into "the old classics" and "the new wave." Like most mature, sophisticated writers and readers, Chaucer was never much worried about whether he should prefer old or new art. He liked and learned from whatever seemed best in both. Still, the classics of French literature, from the 150 years or so before his time, *are* different from the works of his contemporaries, and we may conveniently discuss them separately.

The masterpiece that dominated European vernacular poetry for more than a century was the *Roman de la rose* (Romance of the Rose) and a strange masterpiece it was. It provided a model of style and metaphoric imagination for poets as diverse as Dante and Chaucer. Its status as a classic is incontestable. Dante, having followed his master Vergil through the *Inferno*, the first canticle of his *Commedia*, concludes the third canticle, *Paradiso*, with a canto whose basic metaphor of Christian paradise he derived from the primary erotic metaphor of the *Roman*—the perfect rose.

For all its importance to late medieval vernacular writers, the *Roman de la rose* is not a single poem by a single author. The first four thousand lines or so, by Guillaume de Lorris, were written sometime before the middle of the thirteenth century and are an elaborate, beautifully controlled allegory depicting the psychology of a sexual love that sophisticated, intelligent medieval men and women refused to limit to its purely physical level and converted into a ritual-ceremony-poetry. About forty years later, Jean de Meun—for reasons that no one understands but that will certainly be argued about for many years to come—wrote a more than twenty-two-thousand-line continuation of Guillaume's work, continuing the allegory in an extremely sketchy way, but refocusing the poem entirely away from the psychology of sex and onto its natural, moral, and philosophical status. In the process, he also made space for most of his encylopedic knowledge of the medieval Latin tradition we discussed earlier.

The *Roman de la rose* ranks with Ovid, Boethius, and Boccaccio among the dominant sources of, and influences on, Chaucer's poetry. Chaucer's absorption in it led him, as it had with Boethius's *De consolatione,* to make a translation of it into Middle English. In this case, the vagaries of manuscript survival have left us uncertain how much of the fifteenth-century copies that we now have is really Chaucer's work. In another way, the *Roman's* role as a source for Chaucer seems to have been more like Ovid's *Metamorphoses;* throughout his poetic career he took material from the *Roman* to remake in his own poems and he learned the styles of both its authors thoroughly and modified them for his own use, both the elaborate courtly metaphor of sublimated sex perfected by Guillaume and the discursive, critical, ironic, polemical language of Jean. There is considerable overlap of traditional influence here, too. During the past century, critics have shown us that Jean de Meun's encyclopedic section of the *Roman* could have been Chaucer's introduction to many early and late medieval "authorities," perhaps even including Boethius, whom he later explored on his own. Whatever the order of precedence, both parts of the *Roman* must have confirmed whatever they did not instigate; the classic of thirteenth-century European literature both taught and reassured him of things he was also absorbing from Ovid, Vergil, Boccaccio, Dante, and many others.

Although it is hard to track him to specific works among them, Chaucer had read widely among the thirteenth-century French romances. Four of the surviving twenty-two *Canterbury Tales* are romances and for one of them, the Franklin's Tale, Chaucer claims a French source, although he does not identify it. Throughout his career, his ideas of love and how to depicit it in poetry, as well as his own notions of how to put together an extended fiction, clearly owe much to the romances of thirteenth-century France. And of course

Troilus and Criseyde is a kind of romance, although so transformed by Chaucer's one-of-a-kind poetic imagination as to be finally in a class by itself. One of its principal sources is an even earlier French romance, Benoit de Ste. Maure's mid-twelfth-century *Roman de Troie.* It is evidently Benoit whom we must credit with inventing the story of a love affair between Troilus and Criseyde, and in any case there is clear evidence in Chaucer's poem that he had read Benoit's work.

A very different kind of thirteenth- and fourteenth-century French fiction, the fabliaux, apparently interested Chaucer alone among late medieval English writers. Fabliaux were fast moving, realistic, sometimes farcical stories, often involving slapstick sexual adventures and misadventures, often with bourgeois characters and straying churchmen. Chaucer offers us four such stories in the *Canterbury Tales* and the climactic episode in a fifth, the Merchant's Tale, clearly has its origins in fabliaux. Popular as this type of fiction was in France, Chaucer's are the only ones we have in the Middle English. Indeed, it was a genre that never caught on in England.

As indicated at the beginning of this discussion, Chaucer's contemporaries and near precontemporaries in France were busily transforming the older themes, forms, and genres into a poetry not wholly new and different, but with a character distinctly its own. Guillaume de Machaut in the early and middle years of the fourteenth century, followed by Eustache Deschamps and Jean Froissart in the last half of the century, were creating a highly decorated, artificial, prosodically and metrically superintricate style. This style was to dominate French poetry for the next century and it was a formative influence on Chaucer's work. Its precise and prosodically complex lyrics and ultrarefined and abstracted analyses of love relationships in dream-vision poems largely determined the kinds of things Chaucer wrote in the first half of his career. Indeed, to the end of the *Canterbury Tales,* he continues to write in ways that reflect what he had learned from its practitioners. It is as important for us as tracing Chaucer's imitations of these particular poets[6] to come to see Chaucer, for all his sensitive commitment to the traditional past, much as readers early in the twentieth century saw Ezra Pound or T. S. Eliot, as a poet completely up with and even ahead of his time, in touch with and well-informed about the best of his continental contemporaries and joining them in the vanguard of poetic exploration of his own language.

With regard to the Italians, it is also particularly true that Chaucer was ahead of his time. Although there are vague indications that some of his English contemporaries had read Dante, there is nowhere anything like Chaucer's explicit recognition of him, with occasional direct borrowings. Boccaccio's work was largely unknown and even his name was only slightly known in England for nearly a century after Chaucer. And Petrarch had to wait until well into the sixteenth century for recognition in England and the tribute of widespread imitation.

Much about Chaucer's connections with Italy and Italian literature is tantalizingly uncertain. Despite generations of historical and critical investigation and controversy we will probably never have answers to many of the most important questions. Did Chaucer "discover" Italian literature on his two diplomatic missions to Italy? Or was he sent on those missions because he was already fluent and well read in Italian? Had he actually met Petrarch? Why does he never mention Boccaccio's name? Why did he attribute the source of *Troilus and Criseyde* to a nonexistent Latin poet, Lollius, rather than to Boccaccio? Of one thing we can be sure, however, and that is that the three greatest of the fourteenth-century Italian poets were as important to Chaucer as his French and Latin sources.

Chaucer unmistakably knew well at least one work of Dante's, the *Divina commedia,* and he refers to Dante with great respect and admiration. Yet it is hard to think of two writers more different in style and temperament. Chaucer did little extensive borrowing from Dante—the figure of the eagle in the *House of Fame,* the concluding prayer in *Troilus and Criseyde,* the inscription over the gates in the *Parliament of Fowls,* the Ugolino story in the Monk's Tale—and except for the procrustean "interpretations" of an occasional modern exegete who wants to read Chaucer the way the author of the *Ovide moralise* read the *Metamorphoses,* no one has ever seen much in Chaucer's poetry that could rightly be called Dantean. Still, both were deeply concerned with perfecting their native language into high art; both drew heavily on the poets of ancient Rome, the academic medieval Latin theoreticians, and the love poetry of twelfth- and thirteenth-century France.

As to Boccaccio, things are easier and more obvious for the literary historian. Only Ovid provided Chaucer with more material to remake in his poems. Almost from the beginning of his career, even in the earlier dream poems, Chaucer used extended swatches from Boccaccio's *Teseida,* the *Filocolo,* and the *Filostrato.* And although Chaucer's direct knowledge of the *Decameron* is still uncertain, he did take one of the *Canterbury Tales,* the Clerk's, from it indirectly through a Latin translation made by Petrarch.

It is interesting, however, that unless we wish to argue (as many historical critics are unwilling to do) some kind of affinity in style and tone between the *Canterbury Tales* and the *Decameron,* the poetry Chaucer remakes from Boccaccio is nearly always completely different stylistically from the original. Nowhere is that more evident than in *Troilus and Criseyde* and the Knight's Tale, two masterpieces Chaucer remade from Boccaccian originals. We shall examine both in detail in subsequent chapters, but they should be cited here as typical examples of the kind of use Chaucer made of Boccaccio, as of his other major sources. Chaucer sometimes borrowed large portions of the original, sometimes a whole basic plot. But the borrowed material was combined with other material and assimilated to his own personal style, usually quite altering its psychological and moral values in the process. Also, in the case of *Troilus and Criseyde,* modern scholarship has produced clear evidence that Chaucer also used a French prose version of *Il filostrato, Le roman de Troyle et de Criseide*[7]—a procedure noted earlier in connection with his use of other sources.

Of the third in the triumvirate of fourteenth-century Italians so important to Chaucer, the Clerk of Oxford remarks in the introduction to his tale: "Fraunceys Petrak, the lauriat poete, / Highte this clerk, whos rethorike sweete / Enlumyned al Ytaille of poetrie" (IV:31–33). One judges that Chaucer's feeling for Petrarch was much like the Clerk's; he saw him as a great stylist, an expert in "rethorike sweete"—the moving figurative language and metrical skill that were the primary reason Petrarch's sonnets dominated European lyric poetry. However, we need to be careful here, for the tale introduced with that graceful compliment to Petrarch is from a Latin prose story of the long-suffering saintlike Griselda and Chaucer apparently didn't know that it is actually Petrarch's translation of one of the stories in Boccaccio's *Decameron.* That is, Chaucer knew Petrarch as a writer of serious work in Latin[8] as well as of the famous sonnets to Laura. How he related those diverse performances in a single perception of Petrarch is a question probably beyond the reach of any critic. Anyway, Chaucer did know the sonnets more than a hundred years before any other English poet made any use of them at all. Something of the extent to which Chaucer shared the Clerk's appreciation of Petrarch's "rethorike sweete" is incontestably documented in the first book of *Troilus and Criseyde.*

In a passage labeled in the manuscripts *Canticus Troili* (Song of Troilus), Troilus tries for the first time to express and define his sudden love for Criseyde. Although Chaucer, in the preceding stanza, attributes the song to Lollius, this *Canticus Troili* is in fact a marvelously poetic and reasonably accurate translation of Petrarch's sonnet 88 of the Laura sequence. Chaucer chose not to retain the Petrarchan sonnet form, but it is nevertheless noteworthy that this is the first translation of a Petrarch sonnet into English, a century and a half before Thomas Wyatt and Henry Howard, Earl of Surrey, "discovered" Petrarch and introduced him into England. But I think the most important point about the *Canticus Troili* is the way it confirms the Clerk's judgment of Petrarch's "rethorike sweete." Chaucer's sensitive translation, superbly natural in his very different language, incontestably demonstrates the care with which he learned from the poet who "enlumyned al Ytaille."

Chapter Four

Chaucer's Versification

Everyone who has tried in the classroom to help undergraduates into the delights of Chaucer's poetry has surely wished to be able to state exactly and authoritatively just how Chaucer wanted it to sound when read aloud. At the end of *Troilus and Criseyde,* his finest work, he appeals indirectly to future readers in his envoy to the poem:

> And for ther is so gret diversite
> In Englissh and in writing of our tonge,
> So prey I God that non myswrite the,
> Ne the mysmetre for defaute of tonge.
> And red wherso thow be, or elles songe,
> That thow be understonde, God I biseche!
> (V:1793–98)

The variety of dialects and pronunciations Chaucer was worrying about is of course still with us and no doubt always will be, but modern linguistic study has made it possible to be fairly secure in our knowledge of the basics of how Chaucer's London dialect of Southeast Midland Middle English sounded. What neither he nor any of his contemporaries ever told us with any useful precision, and modern scholars have not helped with it much, is what standard of poetic music Chaucer had in mind by which to measure our possible "mysmeterings" of his verse—our botching of the rhythms he intended us to hear in it.

Throughout his work Chaucer reminds us constantly of his concern for the music of the verse, a music he trusts us to hear, though he does not go so far as Deschamps and Dante and try to explain the linguistic principles on which he built it. Perhaps it is just as well he didn't try, for neither *De vulgari eloquentia* nor *L'art de fere et dictier chancons* tells us much about the inner rhythms or metrical principles of Italian or French poetry. However secure their musical ears were, neither Dante nor Deschamps had a linguistic vocabulary or an analytic system sophisticated enough to explain what they thought they heard in their lines. And with Chaucer we have the additional complication of transposition of a music basic to medieval Romance languages into the basically Germanic (though increasingly romanicized) English.

To be sure, Chaucer was not facing such problems on his own or for the first time. Ever since English poetry began to reemerge slowly and painfully in the late twelfth century from the wreckage the Norman Conquest had caused to Old English culture, English poets had been working to tune their ears and file their tongues to the rhythms and rhymes and closed-stanza structures of their new French exemplars. By Chaucer's time, after two centuries, these originally romance meters must have come to seem perfectly natural to many English poets. Particularly in the lyrics of the fifty years or so before Chaucer's time, English writers produced poems that rate as some of the loveliest in those romance rhythms, though in English they never sound quite the same as their French models.

The underlying difficulty for these early Middle English adapters of French versification was that the French heard the basic beat in the number of syllables to the line. English poets, even long after the collapse of Old English culture, retained some kind of dim auditory memory of the Old English verse line, in which the primary beat consisted of four stressed syllables arranged around a noticeable pause at midline, and with a variable number of syllables per line. In fact, that older kind of verse began to be written again in Chaucer's lifetime, in the English Midlands to the north and west of London, in a distinguished group of poems we now call the "Alliterative Revival." We can illustrate the old Germanic-English meter with a few lines from the opening of one of the best Alliterative Revival poems, *Piers Plowman* (I have marked the stresses with accent marks and the pauses with double slashes):

> I was wéry forwándrit / / and wénte me to réste
> Undir a bróod bánk / / be a bóurne síde,
> And as I láy and lénide / / and lókide on the wátris
> I slómeride into a slépyng, / / it swíghed so mérye.
> (A-Text 7–10)

Even if we read lines 7 and 8 as modern English, the characteristic rocking rhythm comes through clearly: "I was weary from wandering and went to rest / On a broad bank by a brook side."[1] It is important to observe that line 7, read in Middle English, has fourteen syllables; line 8 has eleven; line 9 has fifteen; and line 10 has fifteen. That is, although we hear these lines as more or less of equal length, their length is not a matter of the number of syllables, but of those four stress beats, which are the real measure of the line.

Compare four lines from the opening of the *Canterbury Tales:*

> Whan Zéphirus eék with his swéete bréeth
> Inspíred háth in évery hólt and héeth
> The téndre cróppes, / / and the yónge sónne
> Háth in the Rám his hálve cóurse yrónne. . . .
> (I:5–8)

The alliteration, of course, is gone; more important, line 5 has four stresses, line 6 five, line 7 four, and line 8 five again; only line 7 has a strong midline pause. And—the real clue to Chaucer's French-tuned ear—each line has exactly ten syllables, although we have to make some allowance for the very lightly stressed final *e* on "sonne" and "yronne," what Chaucer's friend Deschamps would have called a feminine rhyme.

The basically syllabic beat, together with the rhymes that bind groups of lines together (in this case, pairs of lines), is what Chaucer's predecessors had been naturalizing in England. After reimmersing himself in French poetry, Chaucer could produce the meter in his verses so naturally that it has sounded to many modern readers like a perfectly indigenous English rhythm.

In a very real sense, the rhythm we hear in Chaucer's lines *is* an indigenous one, although this matter has been debated by modern linguists and critics. Partly because of the natural stress patterns of spoken English and partly because of the surviving feel for the four-stress line, Middle English poets writing eight or ten syllable lines tended to produce, deliberately or not, lines in which stronger and weaker stresses alternate—that is, a meter similar to what, since the middle of the seventeenth century, we have come to call "iambic." Many of Chaucer's lines, including the last three quoted above, read quite naturally that way. But many do not unless we force them with some unnatural pronunciations. If, for instance, we try to read "Whan Zephirus eek with his sweete breeth" as a Dryden-like iambic pentameter, we produce a wrong stress on the last syllable of "Zephirus," and an equally strained shift of stress from the important word "eek" (also) to the preposition "with." Some distinguished Chaucerians in the late nineteenth and early twentieth centuries, convinced that Chaucer always wrote or meant to write regular iambic verse, tried to get around such lines by arguing either that fifteenth-century scribes made mistakes when copying the manuscripts and so spoiled the meters, or that possibly even Chaucer might occasionally have written a bad line.

We may never know exactly what to make of the fact that Chaucer's verses frequently contain iambic rhythms, but it seems preferable for both practical and historical reasons to read them as we would those of his French contemporaries: as fundamentally syllabic lines in which a natural pronunciation produces distinctive rhythmic patterns. In English, those patterns often, but by no means always, sound to us very much like the iambics of later English poetry. But if we let anticipation of such rhythms start to control our reading of Chaucer's lines, we will certainly sooner or later come to grief with lines that are not at all unmetrical but just do not fit that pattern.

At least as important as these basic linear rhythms to our enjoyment of Chaucer's poetry are the various stanza forms (groupings of rhymed lines) that he borrowed, altered, reconstructed, and sometimes invented. For two centuries after his death, until as late as his admirer Edmund Spenser at the end of the sixteenth century, Chaucer was hailed by English poets as a great experimenter with intricate stanzas. By the time of Dryden and Pope, the ten-syllable rhymed couplet Chaucer had apparently invented for the *Legend of Good Women* and then perfected in the *Canterbury Tales* had taken its place beside the blank verse of Shakespeare and Milton as the basic measure for any long poem in English.

Although modern critics have in general not been very kind to the short lyric poems Chaucer composed throughout his life, these works are nevertheless a clear record of his lifelong experimentation with complex and intricate stanza forms, a continuing practice that contributed to his achieving the ease and naturalness of the seven-line rhyme royal stanzas of *Troilus and Criseyde* and the couplets of the *Canterbury Tales*. We may conveniently use the short poems to illustrate some of the rich variety of Chaucer's prosody, but we must remember that except for a couple of very late ones these poems are difficult to date and cannot be said to tell us much about the chronology of Chaucer's development.

In what is perhaps one of his earliest surviving poems, *An A B C,* Chaucer is not only already stretching the eight-syllable line of his French original[2] to the ten-syllable one that will eventually come to seem so basically English. He is also working skillfully with an intricate eight-line stanza, rhymed *a b a b b c b c,* which is quite close to the ottava rima of Boccaccio's *Il filostrato,* the poem Chaucer later remade into *Troilus and Criseyde:*

> Almighty and al merciable queene,
> To whom that al this world fleeth for socour
> To have relees of sinne, of sorwe, and teene,
> Glorious virgine, of alle floures flour,
> To the I flee, confounded in errour.
> Help and releve, thou mighti debonayre,
> Have mercy on my perilous langour!
> Venquisshed me hath my cruel adversaire.
> (1–8)

We need to be very careful with verse like this. Modern readers have mostly lost their taste for this kind of ritual, formal, devotional poetry; the language is stereotyped and formulaic. But there is nothing at all amateurish or uncertain about the prosody itself. All the lincs are good natural decasyllabics; none of the rhymes is forced or strained for. Chaucer already understands the articulation of a relatively long stanza. His first sentence covers exactly the first rhyme sequence, the *a b a b b* part of the stanza. The next sentence, the cry for help, begins with the line that introduces the *c* rhyme and ends on the *b* rhyme which ties it back to the *a b a b b* segment. The last line is a full sentence that completes the pattern by picking up the final *c* rhyme. Notice too those two *c*-rhyme words: "debonayre," the Virgin "of good grace," set against but rhymed with "adversaire," the Devil, who is not only the speaker's enemy, but God's as well.

Artificial though it may sound in that kind of analysis, that is just the kind of sensitive control of prosodic structures that makes Chaucer's best poetry sound so natural and right. Indeed, in another probably early poem in the *balade* form he borrowed from Deschamps, we hear the same eight-line stanza form used with the same sense of its articulation, sounding much like the mature Chaucer of the *Troilus* or the *Canterbury Tales:*

> Nas never pyk walwed in galauntyne
> As I in love am walwed and ywounde,
> For which ful ofte I of myself devyne
> That I am trewe Tristam the secounde,
> My love may not refreyde nor affounde;
> I brenne ay in an amorous plesaunce.
> Do what you lyst, I wyl your thral be founde,
> Though ye to me ne do no daliaunce.[3]

Another of these shorter works, the *Complaint of Mars,* a poem impossible to date with any certainty, illustrates some other interesting things about Chaucer's experiments in prosody. In it, again following French models, he plays with a complex arrangement of stanzas of varying lengths, in a 298-line poem divided into three sections, "The Proem," "The Story," and "The Compleynt." Both Dante and Deschamps analyze such arrangements in their discussions of vernacular verse forms, but Chaucer tried them only in two or three of the minor poems, except for his unfinished *Anelida and Arcite.* There he seems to have intended to use the arrangement in a longer, major work. However, I want mainly to show here the honing of Chaucer's prosodic tools in these very intricate French-derived forms.

The opening stanza of the *Complaint of Mars* is in that seven-line *a b a b b c c* "rhyme royal," which, after the *Parliament of Fowls* and *Troilus and Criseyde,* became inseparably linked with Chaucer's name:[4]

> Gladeth ye foules, of the morowe gray!
> Lo! Venus, rysen among yon rowes rede!
> And floures fressh, honoureth ye this day;
> For when the sunne uprist, then wol ye sprede.
> But ye lovers, that lye in any drede,
> Fleeth, lest wikked tongues you espye!
> Lo! yond the sunne, the candel of jelosye!
>
> (1–7)

The next stanza doubles that first one to fourteen lines, with the rhyme scheme *a b a b b c c d e d e e f f,* and does not reuse any of the rhyme sounds of the first stanza. The third returns to rhyme royal and the next eighteen stanzas (the section marked "The Story") continue in that seven-line form. The section marked "The Compleynt of Mars" switches to a nine-line stanza, rhymed *a a b a a b b c c,* a scheme achieved by doubling the *a*-rhyme lines in the rhyme royal. Then, as he had done in the doubled, fourteen-line second stanza of the poem, so in the first stanza of part IV of "The Compleynt" Chaucer doubles the nine-line stanza to an eighteen-line one rhymed *a a b a a b b c c d d e d d e e f f*.

Probably most modern readers are too far removed from that kind of poetic construction to hear such patterns easily, even after they have been schematically analyzed as I have just done. The analysis itself may seem arcane, far removed from what most of us read or listen to poetry for. But Chaucer's contemporary audience had grown up on that kind of poetry and song and they did expect and appreciate intricate patternings.

All the same, it is fair to point out that Chaucer himself saw the disastrous comic possibilities of getting bogged down in a maze of technical complexities, or of banging them out without subtlety or intonation, like player-piano rolls. In the *Canterbury Tales* he gives to his pilgrim alter ego the wonderfully funny tale of Sir Thopas, which, among its delights, offers us this killing burlesque of one of those tricky stanza patterns:

> Til that there cam a greet geaunt,
> His name was sire Olifaunt,
> A perilous man of dede.
> He sayde, "Child, by Termagaunt!
> But if thou prike out of myn haunt,
> Anon I sle thy steede
> With mace.
> Heere is the queene of Fayerye,
> With harpe and pipe and symphonye,
> Dwellynge in this place."
> (VII:807–16)

These elaborate technical artifices rarely carry over into Chaucer's major poetry, except for the rhyme royal stanza that he chose for all or parts of his best works, *Parliament of Fowls, Troilus and Criseyde,* and four of the *Canterbury Tales*. But the prosodic ease of most of the major poetry is the product of constant practice with demanding fixed forms which these short poems reflect over a period of more than thirty years. It is unfair to Chaucer's lyrics to treat them as mere finger exercises; several are very good poems in their own right. But it is instructive for us to look at them as something like the agility drills a football player goes through in training. They are complicated and artificial, not really much like the maneuvers he will make in a game, but constant practice in them means that the necessary muscular control and confidence will come to him naturally when he needs them.

Chapter Five

Chaucer's Dream Poems

In the Prologue to the *Legend of Good Women* (or the *Seintes Legende of Cupyde,* as the Man of Law calls it in the *Canterbury Tales*), Alceste at one point reads off for the God of Love a bibliography of Chaucer's works up to that point in his career. We are, of course, in the midst of a dream, and some of the works listed either have not survived or were never written. Still, most of the writings Alceste charges Chaucer with do correspond with authentic surviving Chaucerian pieces, so that to the extent to which the Prologue can be dated, it can help us in arranging an approximate chronology of Chaucer's poetic career, a chronology many of the details of which will probably never be established.

There is strong evidence that Chaucer borrowed for this Prologue from Deschamps's *Lai de franchise,* a poem written for the celebration of May Day 1385. Allowing time for Deschamps's poem to have become available to Chaucer and for Chaucer to have made his own version, we can assign a date of approximately 1386 for the first version of the Prologue, that is, a little past halfway through Chaucer's career. Before discussing four of the five major poems that make up the bulk of his production during those sixteen or eighteen years, it will be useful to sketch the outlines of the overall thirty years into which these poems of the first half fit.

Of the pieces Alceste lists as Chaucer's, those we can identify with surviving manuscripts are (in the order in which she lists them), the translation of the *Roman de la rose, Troilus and Criseyde,* the *House of Fame,* the *Book of the Duchess,* the *Parliament of Fowls,* "al the love of Palamon and Arcite," a number of short love lyrics, the translation of Boethius's *De consolatione philosophiae,* and a life of Saint Cecilia. We have good reason to believe that Alceste does not list these works in the order of their composition, but assuming that Chaucer dreamed by the same calendar he lived by, we at least know that all that writing was completed by 1386.

A little reading between the lines tells us a good deal more. Blanche, duchess of Lancaster, who was John of Gaunt's first wife, died in 1368. If, as seems probable, Chaucer wrote his poem commemorating her death within a year or two, it is very likely the earliest of the works listed. And although we are on shakier ground here, the references to *Troilus and Criseyde* throughout the Prologue to the *Legend of Good Women* make it seem to be the most recently finished on the list. The poems and translations in between are of very uncertain date and order; we shall return to that problem later. In any case, we do now have some shape to the picture: his writing career began in 1370 or a little earlier with the *Book of the Duchess* and continued with the other works listed down through about 1385 with the completion of *Troilus and Criseyde.*

What is not listed is important too, in particular the *Canterbury Tales*. Although two stories that eventually were included as Canterbury tales are mentioned by Alceste (the life of Saint Cecelia became the Second Nun's Tale and "al the love of Palamon and Arcite" became the Knight's Tale), it seems apparent that Chaucer had not yet conceived the project of the great framed collection of stories. The conventional wisdom of the past century seems sound: Chaucer probably quickly broke off his unfinished collection of "Seintes legendes of Cupyde" and devoted the last half of his writing career almost exclusively to working on the *Canterbury Tales,* except for some short lyrics and possible revision of earlier work.

During the late nineteenth century, it was usual for Chaucer scholars to see the first half of Chaucer's poetic career, with the exception of *Troilus and Criseyde,* as mainly a time of quasi-slavish apprenticeship, working out skilled but largely unoriginal imitations of his French and Italian masters. However, aside from the fact that the major poems of this period are more imaginative and original than that assessment allows, we must see these first fifteen years as a period of busy experimentation in which the maturing poet moved from short lyrics to complexly framed dream-vision poems to translations to medium-long narratives to whatever generic label we want to put on *Troilus*. A good bit of this work he left unfinished—*Anelida and Arcite,* the *House of Fame,* the *Legend of Good Women*—as he jumped restlessly from project to project, perhaps working on several at once.

Four times in that space of fifteen years, he tried remaking and reconstructing the dream-vision form, producing the group we are to explore in this chapter. At least twice, first in the aborted *Anelida and Arcite* and then triumphantly in *Troilus and Criseyde,* he attempted the long narrative, a great serious love story. So the *Legend of Good Women* became a dividing line in Chaucer's career. Its Prologue is his final try with the reframed dream-vision and it introduces his first try at a large collection of short stories, unsuccessful and unfinished. We see the rest of his life as dominated by a different idea of the collection of tales, the *Canterbury Tales.*[1]

For all the constant experimentation with poetic form and genre and though he was probably sometimes working on more than one project, Chaucer consistently reflected three dominant concerns, three nuclei of formal and imaginative engagement. His involvements with them overlap, and yet they form a rough chronological sequence. The poetic center of the early years is, formally, the framed dream-vision, thematically dominated by the art of love and the art of poetry. In the middle years it is the long, single narrative, exploring human love through the experience of particular characters. Finally, there is the near-total engagement with the large group of stories, held together and interrelated by a framing outer narrative.

Let us begin, then, with the four dream poems: the *Book of the Duchess,* the *House of Fame,* the *Parliament of Fowls,* and the Prologue to the *Legend of Good Women.*[2] Scholars at one time or another have tried to show that all four of them are occasional poems—that is, were written for specific occasions, perhaps by request or on demand. However, no convincing evidence for this interpretation has been offered except for the *Book of the Duchess,* which nearly certainly commemorates the death of Blanche, duchess of Lancaster. Blanche died in 1368 and John of Gaunt remarried in 1372, so we can date this poem with more precision than any other in the group. It is also almost certainly the earliest of them and is generally regarded as Chaucer's first major production.[3]

In it Chaucer establishes a structural pattern that he returns to in each of the other three, and I want to insist on that basic pattern, because it is one of the most original elements in these poems. It has long been a standard judgment among scholars that the dream poems are close (perhaps too close) imitations of the French dream-vision poems from which Chaucer borrowed heavily. The editor of our standard edition of Chaucer's works says in the introduction to the *Book of the Duchess:* "To fulfill the double purpose of the poem Chaucer had the happy idea of adapting a love-vision of the familiar kind to the uses of an elegy. Therein lies the chief originality of the work."[4] Certainly the conversion of a form that had been widely used to analyze and define sexual love into a commemorative elegy is a bold move by the young writer and it proves in the poem to be an apt and tactful one. But Chaucer's poem does not simply reproduce the structural format or the stylistic tone of Machaut's *Jugement dou roy de Behaigne* or Froissart's *Paradys d'amours* or the anonymous *Songe vert,* the fourteenth-century French love visions he used most in making the *Book of the Duchess*.

Those poems, however charming and stylistically sophisticated they may be, are structurally simple. In a few opening lines, the poet, who does not try to give himself any persona, any differentiated identity, falls asleep and dreams the dream that *is* the poem. The dream may consist of a variety of arrangements—debates on the nature of love, allegorical figures giving lectures on the subject, courts in which lovers' cases are tried, etc. Nowhere in Chaucer's modish French exemplars does the dreamer introduce himself, as Chaucer does in the first sixty lines of the *Book of the Duchess,* as a distinct individual with a recognizable speaking voice and some kind of personal experience of his own, outside the dream, that he wants us to hear about. Neither is there anywhere among those continental dream poems anything like what Chaucer does next. Lying in bed before going to sleep to have his marvelous dream, he is reading Ovid's *Metamorphoses* and so he gives us for the next 158 lines a condensed account of Ovid's story of Ceys and Alcione. As has been discussed in chapter 2, this is in part an effort to preserve and re-present something important from the classical past. But more important, he is at the same time articulating into his love-vision elegy another embodiment of the theme of love and loss. Third, in none of the love-visions Chaucer has sometimes been thought to have been constrictively bound to in the early poems does an alter ego of the dreamer appear in any significant way as a participant in the action within the dream. In the *Book of the Duchess* the dreamer is as much a character within the dream as is the Black Knight, the other participant in the dialogue that constitutes the 850-line core of the poem. Finally, although there is a great deal of sophisticated wit and irony in those French love-visions, there is nothing in them stylistically like the undertones (and occasional surface flashes) in the *Book of the Duchess* of that cheerful, self-effacing insouciant humor that Chaucer will develop into a style that has rightly earned him his place as England's greatest comic poet.

We must conclude that in his first major poem, the courtly young devotee of stylish French verse produced a poem original in many ways—ways even more important than his conversion of love-vision into elegy. The basic structure puts a double frame around the central dream: a piece of the poet's own experience and a piece of an old book. Partly by thematic overlap and partly by having the waking narrator reappear as a major participant in the dream, the three-part structure is interlinked as though to imply that all three levels of perception—life experience, books, dreams—are ways of getting at the *sentence,* the inner substance of the poem.

The narrator[5] opens the *Book of the Duchess* by speaking directly and confidentially to us about a "sicknesse," a "melancolye" (medieval psychological terms approximating the modern "neurosis" and "depression") that he has suffered for eight years. It is an enigmatic passage—deliberately so, I think—and its meaning has been much debated. His remark at the end of the passage that "there is phisicien but oon / That may me hele" seems to echo the language of French love lyrics and to imply that the narrator has been involved in an intense and so far unsuccessful love, a kind of indirect suggestion, in a much less painfully final degree, of the paradox of love and loss the Black Knight must confront in the dream.

After that quick, compact reminder that books tell us basic truths about the way the natural world works,[6] the insomniac narrator flips through his Ovid and comes upon an ancient tale of love and loss. It is interesting that Chaucer's retelling considerably darkens the effect of Ovid's tale by omitting the ending in the *Metamorphoses,* where the dead lovers reappear in changed forms. In Chaucer's poem, the story of Seys and Alcione is rather an exemplary one of love and loss, compounding the beauty of Alcione's fidelity with the sorrow of Seys' death and her own self-destruction through grief. At the end, the ghost of Seys, speaking to Alcione, coins a Boethian aphorism that neatly encapsulates one half of the *sentence* of this poem: "To lytel while oure blysse lasteth."

The other half of the sentence—which it would be a serious mistake to undervalue—is that the bliss that cannot endure is very beautiful and of real value while it lasts. It is one principal business of the dream section of the poem to construct for us an image, though one perfected in dream and poetry, of the beauty and value of the ordered courtly life and the ritual of noble love. First, as the narrator dreams he awakens on a fine spring morning in a gorgeous baronial castle, with a typically ritualized medieval hunt just forming outside, he builds for us an image of a civilized world where everything, even hunting game, is ordered by rule and done with style and grace. Then a bit of fairy tale enters with the little puppy who leads the dreamer down a secluded forest path to the secret place, the heart of the woods, where he finds the Black Knight. In the dialogue between the dreamer and the Black Knight that makes up most of the rest of the poem, we are given another, more slowly and elaborately developed image of that ordered, civilized (courtly still seems the best word for it) world. This time, however, it is the kind of love between such civilized men and women that we focus on. Certainly, such love cannot last, as the Black Knight's repeatedly interjected laments for his dead beloved constantly remind us. Still, the dreamer's questions keep prodding the Black Knight's memory into a reconstruction not only of Lady Blanche's beauty, but of the grace and nobility the ordering of their passion had given to their love.

As that reconstructed memory becomes our memorial image of Blanche, it becomes also a part of the Black Knight's consolation. Perhaps the Boethian resignation to mutability and mortality, first stated in Seys's admonitions to Alcione and emergent again at the end of the poem, is the poem's graver consolation, but the way memory keeps alive some of the joy of what has been lost is surely part of it also. All great elegies, I think, work with that paradox. The grieving lament for the dead leads to images that preserve their beauty and joy. That is what the word *memorial* means.

To return to the development of the character of the narrator-dreamer, critics have long debated the appropriateness of the comic touches in the narrator's remarks before the dream and the simple, almost clumsy naïveté of the dreamer in his dialogue with the Black Knight. These are troublesome questions, but perhaps they have obscured an equally interesting matter: Chaucer's experiment with a narrator persona who will guide us through his poems as well as be a figure in them. In this first major work, he is also experimenting, not completely successfully, with a persona whose self-deprecating humor can superimpose upon the serious contents an awareness of comic possibilities in human experience. When he has perfected the technique, as in *Troilus and Criseyde,* it will produce what generations of readers have recognized as characteristic Chaucerian irony, the ability to see human experience from at least two different viewpoints at the same time.

At the beginning of the *Book of the Duchess* we see the narrator-dreamer character as an avid reader of other people's poetry and then briefly at the end as a man trying to write some of his own. In the other three dream poems, that reader-poet complex in the narrator's character, although increasingly comically developed, becomes a major theme and finally the whole, central concern of the Prologue to the *Legend of Good Women*. In the *Book of the Duchess,* the poet half of the complex is minimal, but it is present in the last five lines of the poem, as the narrator awakes with Ovid's book still in his hand:

> Thought I, "Thys ys so queynt a sweven
> That I wol, be processe of tyme,
> Fonde to put this sweven in ryme
> As I kan best, and that anoon."
> This was my sweven; now hit ys doon.
> (1330–34)

Whatever the defects in the *Book of the Duchess,* I do not think they are primarily the result of Chaucer's overdependence on French love-visions. They stem, rather, from the as yet imperfectly realized and controlled possibilities of a complex new kind of remade love-vision just beginning to be formulated. It is a beginning many poets might envy as a mature accomplishment.

The sequence of the next two dream poems, the *House of Fame* and the *Parliament of Fowls,* has been endlessly debated and exact dating will probably never be established. It would be invaluable to know the dates, because then we could see more clearly how Chaucer developed the form he invented for the *Book of the Duchess* into its final version in the Prologue to the *Legend of Good Women.* As it is, we must be content with guesswork and the modern editorial tradition, which is much the same thing. The references in Book II of the *House of Fame* to Chaucer's "rekenynges" seem to place the poem in the years while he was controller of customs, namely, 1374 to 1385. But that is a whole decade and it tells us nothing, for the *Parliament of Fowls* was written during that time too. The main reason most modern editors place the *House of Fame* after the *Book of the Duchess* and before the *Parliament* is, in fact, that the first two are in the French-derived eight-syllable couplet, a meter in which Chaucer never excelled and which he used only in those two works. That is flimsy evidence, but it is the best we have, and I will here follow that sequence.

It might almost be fair to call the *House of Fame* a kind of mock-epic inflation of the reader-poet-dreamer problem into an incomplete, three-book, 2,158-line failure. It might also be fair to call it, as some recent critics have done,[7] the dream poem in which Chaucer first shifted the thematic emphasis to the art of poetry. For nearly a century there have been a few readers who insisted it was neither comic nor concerned with aesthetics, but rather a dark allegory, perhaps of Chaucer's escape from bookish subservience to the French poets into a new realism, or of the flight of his soul toward the perfection of Dante's *Paradiso*.

We might do well to start with the obvious. First, if we simply read the text to mean what it says, the opening 110 lines of the poem are unmistakably Chaucerian comic irony, introducing and simultaneously rejecting a number of established medieval theories about dreams. The second book of the poem is a near masterpiece in the same comic vein, this time giving the treatment to a considerable range of medieval pedagogy; scientific, linguistic, and rhetorical theory; and the narrator's own intellectual and artistic pretentions as well. But most of Book I and all of Book III do not seem to fit. Except for those first 110 lines, all of Book I is taken up with that medievally romanticized retelling of the Dido and Aeneas episode from Vergil's *Aeneid,* as I mentioned in chapter 2. In Book III, the marvelously comic eagle of Book II disappears, and with him most of the irony and stylistic agility. The plodding, mechanical personifications of Fame and the fame seekers are probably all the instruction we need in why Chaucer never again tried his hand at formal allegory.

What we seem to have, then, in the *House of Fame* is a poem that, like the *Book of the Duchess* and the *Parliament of Fowls,* tries to correlate a variety of materials and tones into some kind of ironic perspective. But this time Chaucer seems to have tried to embrace too broad a range and the poem never achieves coherence, despite its flashes of greatness that foreshadow so many good things in his later works.

A kind of pitch is set for the whole poem by the Proem and Invocation to Book I. The Proem opens the work with a breathless, scrambled fifty-line survey of the conflicting variety of medieval dream theories, concluding with a frank admission of the narrator's inability to reduce them to any firm scientific footing:

> But why the cause is, noght wot I.
> Wel worthe, of this thing, grete clerkys,
> That trete of this and other werkes;
> For I of noon opinion
> Nyl as now make mensyon,
> But oonly that the holy roode
> Turne us every drem to goode!
>
> (52–58)

Then, after telling us no one had ever had such a marvelously uninterpretable dream as his, thirty-five lines later, in the Invocation, he lays a dire curse on anyone who does not interpret it accurately:

> And whoso thorgh presumpcion,
> Or hate, or skorn, or thorgh envye,
> Dispit, or jape, or vilanye
> Mysdeme hyt, pray I jesus God
> That (dreme he barefot, dreme he shod),
> That every harm that any man
> Hath had syth the world began,
> Befalle hym therof, or he sterve. . . .
>
> (94–101)

The narrator thus sends us into his poem sharing his enigmatic simultaneous belief in the significance of his dream and skeptical inability to sort out a solid theoretical basis for its interpretation.

That could provide an excellent comic beginning for a burlesque of the pretensions of some of the more ambitious dream-vision poems, particularly Dante's *Commedia*. Several critics have read the poem that way, and there are some borrowings from Dante, particularly in the second book, to support such a reading. Book II of the *House of Fame* is indeed a splendid burlesque, although of many things in addition to the literary conventions of dream visions. However, neither the rest of Book I nor Book III is burlesque at all, or ever funny.

The rest of Book I, after the humorously ironic Proem and Invocation, is a curious piece of work. Instead of the narrator's picking up an old book and summarizing what he was reading in it as he fell asleep, here the old book is moved inside the dream, where it is engraved on a "table of bras" on the walls of the glass temple of Venus, where he finds himself as the dream begins. The dreamer then reads off for us a quite literal Middle English translation of the opening lines of vergil's *Aeneid.* Then follows a rapid summary of the *Aeneid* up to the Dido-Aeneas episode, which is told in more detail and in a curiously twisted, medievalized version, followed by a sketchy summary of the remainder of Vergil's poem.

There are two particularly striking things about Chaucer's style of presenting this Vergilian material. First, starting with lines 149–50, "And tho began the story anoon, / As I shall telle you echon," he seems to forget that he is supposed to be recounting his marvelous dream. For all practical purposes, the dream framework disappears and is replaced by another characteristically Chaucerian rhetorical device, the writer directly addressing his readers about what he is doing and the sources he is using. At line 245, for example, as he begins to tell of Aeneas' love for Dido, he turns directly to his readers (could he do this in a dream?) with the standard author's disclaimer:

> What shulde I speke more queynte,
> Or peyne me my wordes peynte
> To speke of love? Hyt wol not be;
> I kan nat of that faculte
> And eke to telle the manere
> How they aqueynteden in fere,
> Hyt were a long proces to telle
> And over long for yow to dwelle.
> (245–52)

Again at the end of the passage, speaking of Dido's sorrow after Aeneas has left her:

> And al the maner how she deyde,
> And alle the wordes that she seyde,
> Whoso to knowe hit hath purpose,
> Rede Vergile in Eneydos
> Or the Epistle of Ovyde,
> What that she wrot or that she dyde;
> And nere hyt to long to endyte,
> By God, I wolde hyt here write.
> (375–82)

My own guess is that this retelling of the *Aeneid* began as a separate work, as rhetorical machinery of the sort I have just illustrated would indicate, and was moved into the *House of Fame* for reasons that its incompleteness and disjointedness will never allow us to recover.

A second striking feature of Book I seems also to be a confusion in rhetorical procedures, but I think it tells us something interesting about how Chaucer's poetic imagination worked and what he expected poetry to do. At line 151, just after the translation of the opening lines of the *Aeneid,* the dreamer tells us "First sawgh I the destruction / Of Troye. . . ." From that point to the start of the Dido story and resuming immediately after it, "then I saw," "there I saw," and "I saw next" echo at intervals with almost liturgical repetitiveness. It is possible that Chaucer means he saw the lines engraved in the "table of bras" and read them off, but nearly every time the formula introduces a highly visualized representation of a scene in the action. The technique here is very much what we would have expected if Chaucer had detailed what he saw of the *Roman de la rose* in the stained glass windows of the castle he dreamed his way into at the beginning of the *Book of the Duchess.* It is as though the images of great poetry came to life for him, almost literally became images, visually imagined people, actions, and places. The same thing happens for us, his readers, in his great comic poetry of Book II, the wonderfully realized dialogue with the garrulous, pedantic eagle.

As Book I closes, after Chaucer has finished his account of the *Aeneid,*[8] he wanders out of the temple of glass, finds himself in the middle of a desert, and looks up and sees the huge, blazing golden eagle descending upon him.

A number of critics have turned this golden eagle into a red herring. Some of the details of Chaucer's description of him come from Dante's description of his own famous eagle at the beginning of the *Purgatorio.* Similar details also appear in Vergil's and Ovid's descriptions of Ganymede in the form of an eagle. But the real eagle of Book II is the one Chaucer characterizes (in the course of his 550-line dialogue with the timorous dreamer) entirely in terms of his "rethorike"—his studied manner of speaking. The Dantean detail of the twenty or so lines of his introduction in no way determines either the sentence of the whole poem or the way we should read its second book.

What does go on in Book II, the book that in truth is the main reason most people still read the *House of Fame,* is at the same time a development and a refocusing of the issue of the poet of love and his traditional and rhetorical problems and a foreshadowing of those unmatched skills in characterization, versified dialogue, and ideological irony that are the hallmarks of his more famous later poems.

There has been a good deal of sensible and sensitive modern criticism concerning this second book. Here I will merely sketch briefly those qualities in it that link it with the other dream poems and with Chaucer's growing concern, at once serious and comic, for the parallel arts of love and poetry as major themes in these complex visions.

First, the eagle is a rhetorician, a master of instructive and persuasive language. That he is a pedantic and pretentious one complicates but should not obscure the fact, any more than does Chaucer's typically inverted comic confirmation of it as he has the eagle smugly end one of his classroom lectures with

> Have y not preved thus symply,
> Withoute any subtilte
> Of speche, or gret prolixite
> Of termes of philosophie
> Of figures of poetrie,
> Or colours of rethorike?
> (854–59)

Surely the whole topic of this book is the artful use of language. As the eagle first starts to carry the terrified "Geffrey," as he calls him, into outer space, he informs him that the excursion has been ordered by Jupiter in order to improve Geffrey's poetry. The eagle's lecture on the physics of sound, in addition to being a parody of medieval university classroom methods, is also a lecture on how the words of ancient writers echo down through time (from the human point of view) or upward (from Jupiter's point of view) to a kind of permanent filing place in the House of Fame. I said earlier that Book I seems to have little or nothing to do with the rest of the poem, but there may be an indirect connection here. In Book I, the dreamer saw the *Aeneid* immutably engraved in the solid, lasting brass of the wall tablets. But after the eagle explains that

> Soun is noght but eyr ybroken,
> And every speche that is spoken,
> Lowd or pryvee, foul or fair,
> In his substaunce ys but air. . .
> (765–68)

Geffrey can only hear Vergil and Ovid breaking wind down the centuries.

It is important that by the time we have finished with the eagle's lecture, fame (though it will appear personified in the allegory of Book III) has been completely identified with literature—with the written record that preserved whatever fame anyone or anything has in subsequent knowledge and memory. Insofar as the *House of Fame* has a discernible central subject, Book II establishes it as the problem of the meaning of the literary record of the past and what it might teach Geffrey about how to improve his own poetry.

What remains to be emphasized about Book II is the development of its two characters. Already here in an early poem, Chaucer is in full and easy control of stylistic techniques that will be major elements in the success of his later masterpieces. First, there is the perfectly tuned ear for speech rhythms and mannerisms that allows him to make a fully realized comic character of the eagle merely by letting him talk. Different as the later characters may be, there is a lot of Pandarus, Harry Baily, and Chanticleer in this loquacious bird. Then too, there is Geffrey, perhaps for the first time fully developed as a central figure in the poem, the comic, yet still determinedly serious self-characterization of the failed but still trying poet who will figure in all the rest of Chaucer's major works in variously altered guises.

After the comic delights of Book II, the "lytel laste bok" of the *House of Fame* seems repetitious and mechanical and we need spend little time on it here. It opens with an interesting invocation to Apollo, god of poetry, in which Chaucer asserts that in this book he is not trying "to shewe craft," that is, to display his technical virtuosity, but rather just to get across the message, the *sentence*. However, the "o sentence" is a platitude: fame is fickle. The various allegorical restatements of the platitude do little to develop its significance or impact beyond the platitudinous. In fact, there is very little *sentence* in Book III and a great deal of allegorical "craft," most of it labored and obvious. Near the end, just as he is leaving the Palace of Fame, the dreamer-narrator seems to acknowledge that, in an exchange with an unnamed bystander:

> "For certeynly, he that me made
> To comen hyder, seyde me
> Y shulde bothe here and se,
> In this place, wonder thynges;
> But there be no suche tydynges
> As I mene of." "Noo?" quod he.

and I answered, "Noo, parde!
For wel I wiste ever yit
Sith that first y hadde wit,
That somme folk han desired fame
Diversly, and loos, and name."
(1890–1900)

As several critics during the past century have observed, it is hardly surprising, after that, that two hundred lines later the poem breaks off in midsentence with a "man of great auctorite" about to speak in the House of Rumor, a place where there is no way to distinguish truth from illusion or falsehood. Chaucer probably did not know what more to do with his strange, fractured, yet oddly compelling poem and he evidently never returned to it.

The *Parliament of Fowls* is, superficially, Chaucer's poetic valentine for some late fourteenth-century St. Valentine's day occasion whose specific identity is beyond recovery. It is, fundamentally, a major success in the poetic statement of the aesthetic issues at the heart of the *House of Fame,* together with a return to consideration of the nature of human love that characterized the *Book of the Duchess,* and a technically dazzling elaboration and refinement of the comic-ironic style that was becoming the Chaucerian hallmark.

The basic pattern of all the dream poems is here: a bit of the poet-narrator's experience, something from an old book, a marvelous dream—plus the attempt to correlate the three meaningfully. As in the other works with the exception of the *Book of the Duchess,* the dominant stylistic tone is comic, even while we know the seriousness of the issues under consideration. There are also some distinctive features of the *Parliament* that differentiate it from all three of the other dream poems. The most noticeable, especially after the rather constraining octasyllabic couplets of the *Book of the Duchess* and the *House of Fame,* is the polyphonic music of the rhyme royal stanza, which gives the *Parliament* a prosodic panache shared by none of the other three. Especially in the fast-moving debate of the birds, Chaucer brings off a virtuoso performance to match any of his other uses of this elaborate stanza.

There is a distinctive variation of the basic experience-book-dream structure in the *Parliament;* in fact, to one degree or another each of the dream poems varies it. Here, the dream itself consists of two parts, each with a characteristic thematic and stylistic quality, so that the overall structure really has four parts: the narrator's personal introduction, the summary of Macrobius's old book, and the two parts of the dream, each offering a different view of the puzzle of human love.

The poem begins with a stanza that probably tells us, in seven lines, as much about late medieval (especially Chaucerian) ways of imagining love and art as all the scholarly analyses that have been written since:

> The lyf so short, the craft so long to lerne,
> Th'assay so hard, so sharp the conquerynge,
> The dredful joye, alwey that slit so yerne:
> Al this mene I by Love, that my felynge
> Astonyeth with his wonderful werkynge
> So sore, iwis, that whan I on hym thynke,
> Nat wot I wel wher that I flete or synke.
> (1–7)

The opening line, translating the old proverb "ars longa, vita brevis" (art is long, life is short), starts us thinking of the difficulties artists face in perfecting their craft before age robs them of its exercise. The third line, "The dredful joye, alwey that slit so yerne," must surely be one of the most poignantly exact formulations anywhere of the paradoxical mixture of anxiety and exhilaration that artists live with, together with the knowledge that it will all slip away. Then, suddenly, the turn in line 4 that within a half line completely readjusts the perspective: "Al this mene I by Love." Love is also a craft requiring a practiced mastery, a willed and studied rearrangement of the raw materials of nature. The courtly civility of the dreamworld of the *Book of the Duchess* is back for a new consideration.

It would be a wrongheaded introduction to the *Parliament of Fowls* to emphasize that ironic wit without equally pointing up the self-effacing humor of the first stanza's last two lines and the second stanza. Combat soldiers try to ease their fear of death with black, gallows humor; people mask their sexual anxieties in dirty jokes: much humor is a kind of defense, a diminishing and distancing of the immediately worrisome. So the poet-narrator in most of Chaucer's best work regularly laughs at himself for taking seriously things we know—as he did—to be scary matters.

The laughter lasts for only about nine lines. As soon as the narrator has had his joke (an inversion of the witty, serious correlation of the art of poetry with the art of love) about knowing love only from reading books about it, we get two stanzas of elegantly precise statement of what it meant to Chaucer to learn about life and art from the old books:

> Of usage—what for lust and what for lore—
> On bokes rede I ofte, as I yow tolde.
> But wherfore that I speke al this? Nat yoore
> Agon, it happede me for to beholde
> Upon a bok, was write with lettres olde,
> And therupon, a certayn thing to lerne,
> The longe day ful faste I redde and yerne.
>
> For out of olde feldes, as men seyth,
> Cometh al this newe corn from yer to yere,
> And out of olde bokes, in good feyth,
> Cometh al this newe science that men lere.
> But now to purpose as of this matere;
> To rede forth hit gan me so delite,
> That al that day me thoughte but a lyte.
> (15–28)

We should note, too, that planted early in this nice metaphoric blending of the Horatian *dulce et utile* with the medieval Christian concern for drawing new knowledge out of old lore, is that seemingly innocent couplet "And therupon, a certeyn thing to lerne / The longe day ful faste I redde and yerne." This couplet neatly packages most of the anxieties—both serious and comic—seen earlier in the *House of Fame*. All day long the narrator has studied the old book looking for something that would be certain, self-evidently convincing. For all the assurance of profit and delight in the new knowledge that comes from reading his predecessors' works, here is the serpent in Eden. How hard it is to hear what is "certeyn" in those voices of "auctoritee" that the eagle assured Geffrey would always be echoing about in time!

Throughout the rest of the *Parliament of Fowls* we shall be listening to a cacophonous variety of voices, some from old books, some from dreamed characters, each telling us a "certeyn thing." The trouble is that, as with the tips of racetrack touts, each of these certain things is quite different from the others.

As we might expect from the two stanzas quoted above, the first voice we hear is distant, as in an echo chamber: the narrator echoes Macrobius echoing Cicero echoing Scipio Africanus. Even so, as in the similar retelling of the Ovidian story before the dream starts in the *Book of the Duchess,* the moral resonance of the voice, however re-echoed, is clear. Scipio's vision of love is of a quasi-divine principle of harmony and order that holds together the universe and human society. It has nearly nothing to do with the superheated sensuality of the first part of the dream to come, or with the libidinous procreational urge that underlies the debate of the birds in Dame Nature's part of the dream garden.

At the opening of the dream we might note a minor touch that tells us something about how Chaucer is tightening up the structure of his framed vision poems as he goes along. This time the first figure to appear in his dream is the Africanus about whose dream he had been reading in Macrobius. Somewhat like the eagle in the *House of Fame,* Africanus tells the dreamer-narrator that he has come to conduct him into a vision that should improve both his reading of other poets and his own poetry.

> . . . Thow hast the so wel born
> In lokyng of myn olde bok totorn,
> Of which Macrobye roughte nat a lyte,
> That sumdel of thy labour wolde I quyte.
> (109–12)
>
> And if thow haddest connyng for t'endite,
> I shal the shewe mater of to wryte.
> (168–69)

The inscription over the gate to the dream garden, though it is an imitation of the inscription over the gates of Hell in Dante's *Inferno,* nevertheless foreshadows no Dantean horrors. Rather, Chaucer has readjusted his paraphrase so that the double inscription now forecasts just what the dreamer will see in the dream garden: the paradox of the frustrations and fulfillments, the pleasure and pain of sexual love. But before we start to feel that paradox as a kind of Byronic romantic agony, Chaucer's deft comic touch deflates it. The narrator, confused and frightened, freezes before the gate and has to be roughly shoved through by Africanus, thus becoming the first character in literature to be kicked into the enchanted otherworld.

Once inside, he sees what seems at first a paradisal garden of love—the enchanted setting of so many medieval love poems. It is appropriately populated by Cupid and a host of allegorical characters straight out of the *Roman de la rose*. We note, however, that although the dreamer-narrator makes nothing of it one way or another, along with Pleasaunce, Curteysie, Beute, and Youthe, there are also in the garden "Craft that can and hath the myght / To don by force a wyght to don folye," and Foolhardynesse, Flaterye, and Meede (bribery). And as he approaches the Temple of Venus, there are wild, dancing maenads "in kertels, al dishevele." Different as this part of the garden is from Dame Nature's hill of Flowers with squabbling birds, the paradox of love foreshadowed by the inscription over the gates is here too.

The description of the Temple itself and what the dreamer sees inside it draws mainly on Boccaccio rather than the *Roman de la rose,* and the change in tone is marked. The interior is dim and hot, warmed by lovers' sighs and lit by flickering votive fires on the altars of Venus. In passing, the dreamer catches a glimpse of the nearly obscene figure of Priapus, standing just as he had been when caught in the act of rape, "with his sceptre in his honde." Then, describing Venus herself, Chaucer gives us a bit of genuine fourteenth-century soft-core pornography:

> Derk was that place, but afterward lightnesse
> I saw a lyte, unnethe it might be lesse,
> And on a bed of gold she lay to reste,
> Til that the hote sonne gan to weste.
>
> Hyre gilte heres with a golden thred
> Ibounden were, untressed as she lay,
> And naked from the brest unto the hed
> Men myghte her sen; and, sothly for to say,
> The remenaunt was wel kevered to my pay
> Ryght with a subtyl coverchef of Valence—[9]
> There nas no thikkere cloth of no defense.
> (263–73)

And painted on the walls (Chaucer again visualizing his reading matter) are stories of famous lovers, most of them tragic.[10] His last remark as he leaves the Temple is that he had seen "al here love, and in what plyt they dyde."

We almost share the relief of the dreamer's first deep breath of fresh air as he leaves the Temple to "come ayen into the place / That I of spak, that was so sote and grene." Some readers have felt so relieved that they argued that the poem's ultimate *sentence* is that what we see in Dame Nature's part of the garden is the right view of love and that the other images of it are wrong and to be rejected. But the others are certainly there in the same garden that Africanus and the paradoxically inscribed gates had promised the dreamer would show him the truth of love. And Dame Nature's part of the garden is really no such perfectly functioning embodiment of the "lawe of kynde."

It has long been noted that this dream society that Nature, "the vicaire of the almighty Lord," has ordained and rules over is a kind of beast-fable representation of medieval feudal society, although not precisely developed. There are social classes, each with its characteristic style; there is rank and order of precedence; there is conflict, to be resolved by governance. Probably what we see here reflects something of Chaucer's view of fourteenth-century English society and government. Certainly what the dreamer sees and hears in this dream feudal society of birds reflects a conviction Chaucer shared with many satirists, that when real people try to put into practice social and political ideals, the results are more often comic than divine.

Social satire is by no means all that is going on here. Love is still the first order of business, as Dame Nature reminds the birds at the beginning of their "parlement":

> Ye knowe wel how, seynt Valentynes day,
> By my statut and thorgh my governance,
> Ye come for to chese—and fle youre wey—
> Youre makes, as I prike you with plesaunce.
> (386–89)

Despite Nature's statute and governance and the weight of long-established custom, by the time the first aristocratic tersel eagle has finished his plea for the love of the lovely formel eagle perched on Dame Nature's wrist, the orderly process of mating and procreating has already turned into an angry quarrel, which during the rest of the "parlement" will rapidly degenerate into a comic jangle of loudly differing solutions to the problem, all arising out of irreconcilably different notions of what love is and what is the proper pursuit of it. We are many worlds away from the nearly naked Venus in her dimly lighted bedchamber when we reach, late in the birds' quarreling, the duck's pronouncement:

> "Wel bourded," quod the doke, "by myn hat!
> That men shulde loven alwey causeles,
> Who can a resoun fynde or wit in that?
> Daunseth he murye that is myrtheles?
> Who shulde recche of that is recheles?
> Ye quek!" yit seyde the doke, ful wel and fayre,
> "There been mo sterres, God wot, than a payre."
> (589–95)

Or are we? Probably not a whole lot farther than we are from the ideals of the courtly aristocrats whose speeches opened the debate.

At the close of the cacophonous debate, the formel simply refuses to choose, apparently as confused by the clash of ideals and opinions and prejudices as the dreamer had been, standing before the gates to the garden. Dame Nature herself, "vicaire of the almighty Lord, / That hot, cold, hevy, lyght, moyst, and dreye / Hath knyt by even noumbres of accord," has to give up and declare it an impasse beyond her control or powers of arbitration.

> "Now, syn it may non otherwise betyde,"
> Quod tho Nature, "heere is no more to seye.
> Thanne wolde I that these foules were aweye,
> Ech with his make, for tarrying lengere heere!"
> (654–57)

Instantly, the order Nature had previously been unable to maintain among the birds reasserts itself—surely a miraculous conclusion, in no way a logical consequence of what had gone before. And as the dissonant wrangling of the birds quiets into the harmony of their concluding song, Chaucer has with us perhaps his subtlest joke of the poem:

> But fyrst were chosen foules for to synge,
> As yer by yer was alwey hir usaunce
> To synge a roundel at her departynge,

> To don to Nature honour and plesaunce
> The note, I trowe imaked was in Fraunce,
> The wordes were swiche as ye may heer fynde,
> The nexte vers, as I now have in mynde.
> (673–79)

The birds in Nature's own garden are finally able to sing harmoniously only after borrowing the artificially ordered music of the French poets. And their song, as Chaucer writes it, breaks the rhyme royal pattern and reproduces an intricate *roundel* pattern that is close to both Machaut and Deschamps.[11] At the end, the dreamer awakens to his own books and poetry again, leaving the puzzling vision of the garden of love for us to make of it what we can.

Whatever the chronology of the three dream poems so far considered, we can be fairly certain that Chaucer's last reworking of the framed dream vision was written a little after the mid-1380s. In order to treat all four of these related poems together, I am breaking the known chronological order and postponing to the next chapter a discussion of *Troilus and Criseyde,* a poem he had clearly just finished before writing the Prologue to the *Legend of Good Women*. There is an additional problem about the Prologue, partly involving dating, but it need not trouble beginning Chaucerians, and persons interested in learning more about it can easily do so by pursuing references in notes to good modern editions of Chaucer's works. This difficulty arises from the survival of two distinctly different versions of the Prologue, usually called the "F" version and the "G" version. Although the "G" version survives in only one manuscript, there is little doubt that both are Chaucer's work. He obviously made a thorough revision of the Prologue,[12] but we remain uncertain of the direction in which he was revising. That is, which of the two versions is the earlier (presumably around 1386) and what might be the date of the later version?

The question has been hotly debated, but the most telling bit of evidence seems to indicate that the "G" version was the revision and that it was made sometime after 7 June 1394, when Queen Anne died. Near the end of the "F" version, Alceste commands the dreamer-poet: "Goo now thy wey, this penaunce ys but lyte. / And whan this book ys maad, yive it the quene, / On my behalf, at Eltham or at Sheene" (495–97). The parallel passage in the "G" version reads simply, "Go now thy wey, thy penaunce is but lyte" (485). That is, the reference to Queen Anne and two of the principal residences she shared with King Richard II have disappeared. Contemporary records tell us that at Anne's death, the emotionally unstable Richard went into a neurotic depression, had the palace at Sheen destroyed, and for a time forbade the mention of her name in his presence. That was surely reason enough for the deletion of the two lines from "F," and strongly suggestive that sometime in the mid-1390s, while he was presumably deeply engaged with the *Canterbury Tales,* Chaucer returned to the Prologue to the *Legend of Good Women* for a thorough revision of his last framed dream vision.

Before we discuss it, something needs to be said about the fact that it is a prologue, the introduction to Chaucer's first attempt at a large collection of stories. The simple existence of the *Canterbury Tales* all but forces upon us what is probably an unfair comparison. The nine legends Chaucer wrote before abandoning the project (he actually breaks off before the end of the ninth, the legend of Hypermnestra) do not bear comparison with most of the surviving twenty-two *Canterbury Tales* as narrative poetry. Most of them seem more like sketches or story outlines than fully worked-out narratives. And, unlike the General Prologue to the *Canterbury Tales,* the Prologue to the *Legend of Good Women* introduces no fiction to serve as a frame around, and links between, the tales. Had the nine legends happened to get separated and to survive only in an independent manuscript, we would not guess they had ever had a general introduction of any kind, let alone anything like the two versions of the Prologue we now have. One thing, however, must be said for the legends. In them Chaucer continues to perfect what he had begun in the Prologue, his control of the ten-syllable rhymed couplet, which as far as we know he invented for this poem, and which he continued to use for most of the *Canterbury Tales.* Largely because of the influence of the latter, the measure came to seem to later writers the quintessential English narrative meter.

To return to the Prologue,[13] the first thing to be said about the last of the dream poems is that in it the seriocomic figure of the narrator-dreamer who is a struggling poet of love becomes the central figure of the poem, the protagonist in the dream as well as the speaker in the predream section. Here, even more than in the second book of the *House of Fame,* this narrator-dreamer-poet closely resembles the historical Geoffrey Chaucer.

In the 88-line introduction, before the dream begins, the experience and old book segments of the frame are fused. The narrator talks to us about how old books extend our experience beyond the immediate possibilities of mortally limited time and space:

> A thousand sythes have I herd men telle
> That there is joye in hevene and peyne in helle,
> And I accorde wel that it be so;
> But natheles, this wot I wel also,
> That there is non that dwelleth in this contre,
> That eyther hath in helle or heven ybe,
> Ne may of it non other weyes witen,
> But as he hath herd seyd or founde it writen: . . .
> ....
> Thanne mote we to bokes that we fynde,
> Thourgh whiche that olde thynges ben in mynde,
> And to the doctryne of these olde wyse
> Yeven credence, in every skilful wyse. . . .
> (1–20)

There is a subtle irony here that reminds us of the more obvious irony of the second book of the *House of Fame:* which of the voices speaking to us from the past do we trust? How do we verify the accuracy of someone else's report of what only he has experienced? The narrator fails to develop that irony, but rather turns it back upon himself as a poet.

Shortly after the lines quoted above, the narrator reports that he likes to leave his books on fine May mornings to walk in the fields and admire the daisies, whose surpassing beauty compels his poetic praise:

> This dayesye, of alle floures flour,
> Fulfyld of vertu and of alle honour,
> And ever ylike fayr and fresh of hewe,
> As wel in wynter as in somer newe,
> Fayn wolde I preysen, if I coude aryght;
> But wo is me, it lyth nat in my myght!
> (55–60)

Such perfect beauty, whether in a flower or in a person, is probably always beyond any writer's might, but the following lines assure us that this writer will nevertheless give it his best try. As we may by now expect, he will seek help in the task from the old books, and so he says in a nice reprise of the old fields and new corn metaphor drawn from his own earlier *Parliament of Fowls:*

> For wel I wot that folk han here-beforn
> Of makyng ropen, and lad awey the corn;
> And I come after, glenyng here and there,
> And am ful glad if I may fynde an ere
> Of any goodly word that they han left.
> (61–65)

As the narrator conducts us into his dream this time, although we notice much in the landscape that is like the enchanted dream gardens of the *Book of the Duchess* and the *Parliament of Fowls,* including birds singing in praise of St. Valentine, the relation of the dreamworld to the waking one is far closer. This dream meadow is different only in degree from the one the waking narrator had wandered in; and—although here the degree of difference is of enormous importance—Alceste in the dream is a transformation of the earlier daisy, a kind of Ovidian metamorphosis that Chaucer apparently invented for this poem.

With the appearance in the garden of the God of Love and the perfect love object, Alceste, with her daisylike crown of pearl, the poem seems to move closer to the earlier French love visions Chaucer had used before. We almost expect the garden to turn into a court of love in which the God of Love and Alceste may sit as judges of a debate over some question of *fin amor*. The dream does turn into a kind of trial, but it is a trial of Chaucer the love poet and the question to be judged is the quality of his poetry, not the courteous refinement of his love. Alceste, furthermore, becomes not a judge but the intercessor for the defendant.

After a charming scene of the lovely ladies ring-dancing around the daisy while singing a *balade* in praise of Alceste, the God of Love spots the dreamer "lenynge faste by under a bente," and promptly charges him with writing bad love poetry. The remainder of the dream is occupied with the perennial argument—one still very much with us—over what writers intend and what various readers and critics make of their work. Chaucer's comic irony keeps the worrisome problem fairly well distanced here, though we might recall that it is essentially the same problem he dealt with quite seriously in the introductory 88 lines. There is irony in the God of Love's imperceptive reading of *Troilus and Criseyde* (can a god be wrong?), though his declaration that the *Roman de la Rose* is a heresy against love might be understandable if applied only to Jean de Meun's part of the poem. Still, the issue is there: do poets sometimes write more or less than they mean to? What authority does the reader's interpretation of a poem have? How much do good intentions count? The narrator-dreamer-poet seems to offer his good intentions as his only defense: "Algate, God wot, it was myn entente / To forthere trouthe in love and it cheryce . . ." (461–62). And Alceste, having reported that very useful list of Chaucer's works to date, pleads only that he will not do it again and asks the God of Love to be merciful, as a proper god ought to be.

The Prologue ends, a bit ironically, with Alceste assigning Chaucer, as penance for his bad love poetry, the task of writing more love poetry. With all the puzzles of the love poet's craft still unsolved, our final image of the dreamer poet is of him picking up his pen to start yet another poem, this one the failed experiment in a new kind of collection of narratives, but a failure that will lead him on to one of his greatest successes, the *Canterbury Tales*.

Chapter Six
Troilus and Criseyde

We must now go back to consider the poem the God of Love thought was one of Chaucer's greatest sins against him and which most readers since have thought the greatest love poem in our language. Sir Philip Sidney, that perceptive and demanding sixteenth-century critic, found it the only poem among his English predecessors that he cared to mention in the company of Homer and Vergil. Although for two centuries after Sidney the *Canterbury Tales* preempted most of the attention given to Chaucer, twentieth-century readers and critics have been increasingly inclined to return *Troilus and Criseyde* to the status Sidney gave it.

Like the other Chaucer poems we have considered, *Troilus and Criseyde* draws heavily on the old books, in this case a traditionally established story that can be traced from its rudimentary beginnings in the fourth- and fifth-century accounts of the Trojan War, through various retellings, down to Chaucer's immediate source, Boccaccio's *Il filostrato* and a French prose version of the latter, *Le roman de Troyle et de Criseyde,* which Chaucer also used. The Troy story had long held the imaginations of medieval readers and writers and enjoyed a special vogue during Chaucer's lifetime. Besides Chaucer's own poem and *Il filostrato* and its French translation, there is the long, and frequently very effective *Geste Hystoriale of the Destruccioun of Troye,* an alliterative poem by an anonymous English contemporary of Chaucer's, and John Lydgate's early fifteenth-century *Troy Book*.

The story of the love affair between Troilus and Criseyde, however, has a separate history from that of the Troy legend in general, and we should take a little time to outline it here, since Chaucer had done his homework carefully and made at least some use of all the earlier sources we know about. The names of most of the characters appear in Homer's *Iliad,* but medieval readers had little or no direct knowledge of that poem, and in any case Homer gives no hint of any love story. That elaboration of what happened during the siege of Troy is a strictly medieval development, although medieval readers seem to have felt sure it properly belonged among the classical historical accounts.

Two early Latin accounts of the Trojan War, one in the fourth century purportedly by Dictys Cretensis and another in the fifth century that claims to be a translation of an account by the Trojan priest Dares Phrygius, give us the names and brief descriptions of Troilus and Criseyde. Neither mentions any connection between them. It was apparently the French poet Benoit de St. Maure, a little past the middle of the twelfth century, who invented the love story, interspersing it segmentally to provide digressions from the battle scenes in his *Roman de Troie,* a long account of the war. About a century later, the Italian Guido delle Colonne, without bothering to acknowledge the source, clad Benoit's *Roman* in the academic dignity of Latin prose in his *Historia Troiana,* a work that remained until Milton's time a standard source for Trojan history. It seems likely that Chaucer and his contemporaries, after reading Guido, took the Troilus story to be history as well as romance.

It was Giovanni Boccaccio who, not long before Chaucer was born, picked the love story out and gave it an independent status, fictionalizing it almost completely in his *Il filostrato* by setting it in a Troy that is transparently a fourteenth-century Italian city and telling us in his introduction that it is to be read as a kind of metaphoric account of what he felt was the betrayal of his love by his beloved Fiametta.[1] The result is a long-suffering and long-lamenting young Troilus; an opportunistic, amorous, and willing Criseyde; and a Pandarus of their own age (in Boccaccio he is Criseyde's cousin) who is mainly an urbane, slightly cynical procurer and arranger of assignations.

Before considering Chaucer's use of Boccaccio's poem, there is a problem to be mentioned briefly and then put aside. All of the sources and versions of the Troy and Troilus story I have mentioned are acknowledged by Chaucer (though not always at the time he uses them) except one, the immediate and principal source of his poem, *Il filostrato*. Early in Book I, in the first specific acknowledgment Chaucer makes of any source, he attributes it to a Roman author whom no one has ever been able to identify: "And of his song naught only the sentence, / As writ myn auctour called Lollius" (I:393–94). Generations of young academics seeking promotion and seasoned veterans who cannot put down an unsolved puzzle have tried to find out why Chaucer never mentions Boccaccio by name and what was this source by a presumably Roman author whose name he thought was

Lollius. For more than a century we have known beyond question that Chaucer knew and used a text of *Il filostrato* in its original Italian. Why is it not acknowledged along with other sources, even if Chaucer did not know Boccaccio's name? As we have already seen, he is never reluctant to acknowledge sources; using sources and acknowledging them is part of what he considered standard poetic practice. Since we are not likely to solve this mystery, we shall not linger longer over it here.

A quick comparison between *Il filostrato* and *Troilus and Criseyde* makes it possible to infer from Chaucer's changes in his immediate source where he wanted his own poem to go. First, a few statistics may prove instructive. *Il filostrato* is 5,704 lines long, composed in eight-line ottava rima stanzas very like the eight-line stanzas Chaucer used in some of the minor poems we looked at in chapter 4. Of the 5,704 lines, Chaucer reused (in more or less exact translation) 2,750 lines in *Troilus and Criseyde.* But because Chaucer's usual practice in this case is to translate each of Boccaccio's eight-line stanzas with one of his own seven-line rhyme royal stanzas, he comes out with 2,580 lines of Boccaccian origin. That is, before he began to rebuild it into his own poem, Chaucer condensed *Il filostrato* to about 45 percent of its original length. The version of *Troilus and Criseyde* that most modern editors print is 8,239 lines long, or about 2,500 lines longer than *Il filostrato;* simple subtraction shows that what Chaucer added to what he had condensed out of the source constitutes about as many lines as it had in the first place. Or to put it a little differently, a simple line count shows that what is directly traceable to *Il filostrato* constitutes a little less than a third of the finished *Troilus and Criseyde*.

In the main, what these figures tell us is that Chaucer boiled off from Boccaccio's poem nearly everything but its basic story and then rebuilt on that plot a wholly new poem. Among the major changes in effecting that new poem, changes not to be measured by line counts, are first of all the complete recharacterizations of both Criseyde and Pandarus; second, the freeing of the character of Troilus from its semi-allegorical function as a representation of the author; and, finally, the creation of a new persona for the author, one closely related to the narrator-dreamer of the dream poems and wholly unlike anything in Boccaccio or in any of Chaucer's other sources. In obvious consequence, the *sentence* of Chaucer's poem is radically altered also.

One surface indication of the changed character of the poem is the new structure Chaucer gave it; he divided it into books in the manner of serious Latin epics and provided each book except the last, Book V, with a stylistically elaborate proem. Medieval theorists associated these procedures with the "high style" they thought appropriate to the most serious and elevated themes and moral considerations and to the most ambitious poetic enterprises. The poem ends with a formal envoy committing the poem to future ages and with a sonorous, formally elaborate prayer. It is true that in many of Chaucer's authorial interventions in the poem, the familiar self-deprecating irony of his persona undercuts such high seriousness; and he casts a comic light over much of the action. Yet there is no doubt that ultimately he means his poem to be taken seriously. He means it when, just before the concluding prayer, he wishes his book to take its place with "Virgile, Ovide, Omer. Lucan, and Stace."

Just as nature is said to abhor a vacuum, there is a certain kind of literary critic who cannot stand an ambiguity, so there has been a lot of debate over what to do about the unmistakable presence in Troilus and Criseyde of both the high seriousness and the high comedy. The effort to decide whether the sorrow in the poem cancels out its gladness or vice versa seems to me ill considered. The laughter and tears, the pain and joy, simply are both there. If we attend carefully to the modulations in the tone of the narrator's comments to his readers as we move through the poem, we will find ourselves constantly maneuvered back and forth between almost sentimental concern and tolerant amusement, between a detached moral objectivity and an immediate human empathy with the characters. The general perspective of the poem, in fact, has sometimes been characterized as "middle-aged," the outlook of a somewhat scarred survivor of youth and love who can look back on it with a mature mixture of sympathetic understanding and evaluative objectivity.

Right at the beginning of the poem we encounter this shifting about of tone and perspective. Chaucer starts by announcing that he will tell us of Troilus's sorrow and invokes the Fury Thesiphone to guide "Thise woful vers, that wepen as I write." But after two stanzas in that vein we are abruptly brought down from that severe classical altitude:

> For I that God Loves servantz serve
> Ne dar to Love, for myn unliklynesse,
> preyen for speed, al sholde I therefore sterve,
> So fer am I from his help in derknesse.
>
> (I:15–18)

The timorous, humble outsider of the dream poems is back again, trying to bumble his way through to a truth he has not the experience to understand. The disclaimer is a bit suspect, however, when we notice that its opening line is phrased in a parody of the papal signature, "Servus servorum dei" (servant of the servants of God). And at line 22, "But ye loveres, that bathen in gladnesse," a second invocation begins, this one to lovers bathed in happiness. Through the following four stanzas, the narrator invokes alternately the joys and the sorrows of love.

We will hear that sort of alternation of tone (and consequently of levels of seriousness) in different ways throughout the poem. Sometimes it will occur directly, as an abrupt shift in style of speech, as it does in the opening of Book I. In Book II, for instance, as Criseyde is about to go to bed and dream the dream that will reveal her love for Troilus, the narrator tells us:

> The dayes honour, and the hevenes yë,
> The nyghtes foo—al this clepe I the sonne—
> Gan western faste, and downward for to wrye,
> As he that hadde his dayes cours yronne;
> And white thynges wexen dymme and donne
> For lak of lyght, and sterres for t'apere,
> That she and alle hire folk in went yfeere.
>
> So whan it liked hire to go to reste,
> And voided weren thei that voiden oughte,
> She seyde that to slepen wel hire leste.
> Hire wommen soone til hire bed hire broughte.
> Whan al was hust, than lay she still and thoughte
> Of al this thing; the maner and the wise
> Reherce it nedeth nought for ye ben wise.
>
> (II:904–17)

The passage opens with a metaphoric description of the setting sun that looks as though it means to proceed in the high style. But as three epithets for the sun pile quickly atop each other, the lines become a burlesque of that style, and Chaucer tips the joke by remarking that all that fancy language merely means the sun. Yet immediately, in the rest of the stanza, the narrator gives a wonderfully delicate description of the gathering dusk which at once restores a serious, almost sentimental mood. This mood continues through the next stanza, with Criseyde's ladies helping her prepare for bed, then leaving her alone in the now stilled and darkened bedchamber. It would be hard to imagine a more romantically set scene for Criseyde's fateful dream. But the narrator then barges in with that last couplet, to elbow us in the ribs and reassure us confidentially that he knows all us veterans of love know what goes on in the mind of a beautiful woman in bed thinking about a handsome young man. So we are jerked out of the scene and made to view it, with some amusement, from a greater distance.

Sometimes Chaucer manages a similar effect not by direct intervention of the narrator's speaking voice, but by skillful management of the action itself. In the complex, climactic scene in Book III, Troilus and Criseyde meet in Pandarus's bedchamber to consummate their love. Throughout the scene, the narrator gives full and serious representation to the beauty and tenderness of the lovers and their feelings. But all the while, Pandarus is busying around the edges of the scene, rushing in with a cushion for Troilus to kneel on at Criseyde's bedside, coaching the lovers on what to do next, all but throwing Troilus into bed, and finally leaving with a wisecrack after having almost—but not quite—turned the scene into a farce:

> Quod Pandarus, "For aught I kan aspien,
> This light, nor I, ne serven here of nought,
> Light is nought good for sike folkes yën!
> But, for the love of God, syn ye ben brought
> In thus good plit, lat now no hevy thought
> Ben hangyng in the hertes of yow twey"—
> And bar the candele to the chymeneye.
> (III:1135–41)

No amount of social history informing us about the general lack of privacy in medieval houses, even in aristocratic bedchambers, can obscure the fact that we must see this central episode in the poem simultaneously as high medieval sentimental romance and as sexual comedy.

Later in the poem, as the comic view disappears, the multiplicity of perspectives involves us in different issues, particularly the narrator's determination to maintain our sympathy for Criseyde even as he must show us the moral and psychological gravity of her betrayal of

Troilus. This changed divergence of perspectives begins to show up early in Book IV:

> For how Criseyde Troilus forsook,
> Or at the leeste, how that she was unkynde,
> Moot hennesforth ben matere of my book,
> As writen folk thorugh which it is in mynde.
> Allas! that they sholde evere cause fynde
> To speke hire harm, and if they on hire lye,
> Iwis, hemself sholde han the vilanye.
> (IV:15–21)

It is, I think, not at all too great a wrenching of this text to find a subtext beneath it. The narrator's moral dilemma catches him between his human love and understanding of his characters and his moral certainties about their actions. His historical dilemma catches him between his commitment to his texts and his uncertainties, after all those years, about whether they speak clearly or he hears rightly. And those of us who have paid close attention to Chaucer's devotion to Boethius may well hear echoing behind a passage like this one, Boethius's "But it is hard for me to recount all this as if I were a God for it is not fitting for men to understand intellectually or to explain verbally all the dispositions of the divine work."[2]

That is, in fact, a Boethian sentiment Chaucer had also distantly echoed at the very beginning of the poem: "O blynde world, O blynde entencioun! / How often falleth al the effect contraire / Of surquidrie and foul presumpcioun" (I:211–13). From the beginning of this poem, we are in a world governed by two certainties: there are immutable laws, and no mortal will ever truly know them. It is one thing to know, as the slightly offensively self-righteous narrator does in the lines following those just quoted, that "This Troilus is clomben on the staire, / And litel weneth that he moot descenden; / But alday faileth thing that fooles wenden." These are good solid Boethian sentiments: Fortune rules the fallen world, and only fools ever expect to beat the game. It is something else again to know the equally Boethian precept spelled out (with a good deal more human sympathy) in the following stanza—all men born into this world are constrained by the "law of kynde" (the natural order of things) to play the game:

> As proude Bayard gynneth for to skippe
> Out of the weye, so pryketh hym his corn,
> Til he a lasshe have of the longe whippe;

> Than thynketh he, "Though I praunce al byforn
> First in the trays, ful fat and newe shorn,
> Yet am I but an hors, and horses lawe
> I moot endure, and with my feres drawe;"
>
> So ferde it by this fierse and proude knyght:
> Though he a worthy kynges sone were. . . .
> (I:218–26)

For the narrator of *Troilus and Criseyde,* that "lawe of kynde" so binds him in human sympathy to his characters that he seems constantly to be fighting off the moral judgments their actions demand. How hard it is—and what a pity—that we should finally have to judge the lovely Criseyde harshly! The narrator is even willing to hope, though he knows better, that maybe the record is wrong and some of the old writers lied about her. Much later, in the last book, he is still struggling with that divided commitment, much like the dreamer before the gates of the garden of love in the *Parliament of Fowls,* paralyzed "Right as betwixen adamauntes two / Of evene myght, a pece of yren set / Ne hath no myght to meve to ne fro—":

> Ne me ne list this sely womman chyde
> Forther than the storye wol devyse.
> Hire name, allas! is punysshed so wide,
> That for hire gilt it oughte ynough suffise.
> And if I myghte excuse hire any wise,
> For she so sory was for hire untrouthe,
> Iwis, I woulde excuse hire yet for routhe.
> (V:1093–99)

The changing voices in which we are addressed by this fussy, self-deprecating, worried, but still determinedly pedagogical narrator who seems to see everything from at least two contradictory points of view is the primary strategy Chaucer uses to control our responses to his poem. But there are other important strategies at work, too, one of the most important of which (and closely related to what we have just been discussing) is what one of the best of our contemporary interpreters of Chaucer's work has called his double vision: the way the narrator sometimes sees the action as completed, far past and known, the stuff of history and old books; and sometimes as dramatically present, live, current experience, in process, immediate, and emotionally exigent.[3]

The opening of the poem gives us a kind of vignette version of that procedure and a foretaste of the way much of the rest of the narrative presentation will be managed. After the invocations, Chaucer begins at line 57 ("It is wel wist how that the Grekes, stronge / In armes, with a thousand shippes, wente / To Troiewardes . . .") several stanzas of generalized summary of the historical accounts of the background to his story, pausing to emphasize Calkas's desertion to the Greeks, leaving his beautiful daughter Criseyde behind in Troy, and finally concluding this summary with a typical referral to his sources:

> But how this town com to destruccion
> Ne falleth naught to purpose me to telle;
> For it were here a long digression
> Fro my matere, and yow to long to dwelle.
> But the Troian gestes, as they felle,
> In Omer, or in Dares, or in Dite,
> Whoso that kan may rede hem as they write.
> (I:141–47)

A stanza later, a particular scene begins to come into focus, the one in which the fatal main action of the story will be generated, though it is still seen from some distance as a kind of tableau painted in the familiar colors of medieval romance:

> And so bifel, whan comen was the tyme
> Of Aperil, whan clothed is the mede
> With newe grene, of lusty Veer the pryme,
> And swote smellen floures white and rede,
> In sondry wises shewed, as I rede,
> The folk of Troie hire observaunces olde
> Palladiones feste for to holde.
> (I:155–61)

Then the conventional opening scene of many a medieval romance dissolves into the circumstantial action and dialogue of this particular story. Criseyde enters quietly and stops near the door, followed by Troilus and his retinue of young knights, strutting the aisles and laughing and talking as they ogle the girls. Then abruptly, just as we have begun to catch a character for Troilus from the manner of his speech, the narrator breaks off the scene with a seven-stanza moral lecture on the dangerous pride and self-delusion of bantering young bachelors who think themselves immune to the power of love.

At line 267, the scene is resumed, again in such circumstantial detail and dramatic immediacy that we visualize it almost as played out on a stage. Even so, there is a literary tone that some of Chaucer's contemporary audience may have caught; many of his modern readers have done so. This scene, as the crowd in the temple momentarily parts and Troilus glances through straight into Criseyde's eyes so that "sodeynly he wax therwith astoned," is a direct imitation of the famous scene in the *Vita nuova* in which Dante first sees and falls in love with Beatrice. The dramatic immediacy is sustained as Troilus later returns to his own room and sits, turning over in his mind what has happened to him, but it is broken off anew by the narrator's interruption to return our attention to his literary sources and his own writing:

> And of his song naught only the sentence,
> As writ my auctour called Lollius,
> But pleinly, save oure tonges difference,
> I dar wel seyn, in al that Troilus
> Seyde in his song, loo! every word right thus
> As I shal seyn; and whoso list it here,
> Loo, next this vers he may it fynden here.
> (I:393–99)

All through the poem, Chaucer maneuvers us up close to and back away from its action like a movie director managing his cameras, though that comparison is too limited. Chaucer does it all with language and its skilled management, a far more difficult achievement than planning camera positions. The scenes in which we are brought so close to the action as to be empathically involved in it do constitute the bulk of the poem, and it is a fundamental mistake to undervalue them. At the same time, they are so compelling that a good many readers have become so engaged in them as to argue that they constitute the "real" poem Chaucer meant to write and that the outer perspective, the other narrator's voice, is some kind of medieval mistake for which we have to forgive Chaucer.

Nevertheless, those compelling scenes, those parts of the poem that, like the painted windows of the castle in the *Book of the Duchess*, play out before our eyes and in our hearts what is happening, make up the bulk of the poem. They remain for all of us a dominant in the emotional impression we carry away from it. And they are not like anything else in medieval poetry. In them Chaucer perfects the kind of dialogue he had begun to experiment with in the *Book of the Duchess* and had developed so strikingly in the second book of the *House of Fame* not only into a mode of precise characterization, but into a registration of a whole social milieu as well.

We pick up this procedure early in the poem, after Pandarus has discovered Troilus's love; the dialogue between the two begins simultaneously to differentiate their characters and to define their two widely differing attitudes toward love. Troilus's confession of his love to Pandarus, echoing the Petrarchan conceits of the *Canticus Troili* 200 lines earlier, confirms the unbending idealistic courtly style we are to hear from Troilus throughout the poem:

> Than gan this sorwful Troylus to syke,
> And seide him thus: "God leve it be my beste
> To telle it the; for sith it may the like
> Yet wol I telle it, though myn herte breste,
> And wel woot I thow mayst do me no reste;
> But lest thow deme I truste nat to the,
> Now herke, frend, for thus it stant with me.
>
> "Love, ayeins the which whoso defendeth
> Hymselven most, hym alderlest avaylleth,
> With disespeyr so sorwfulli me offendeth,
> That streight unto the deth myn herte sailleth.
> Thereto desir so brennyngly me assailleth,
> That to ben slayn it were a gretter joie
> To me than kyng of Grece ben and Troye."
> (I:596–609)

Indeed, most of the elaborate metaphoric language in the poem comes in Troilus's speeches. Nearly always, his is the language of French love poetry, and to the extent that we identify him with the romantic idealism of that poetry he becomes the most conventional character in the poem, the most literary, the least realistic. This may be why many readers feel him to be the least sophisticated. To some he even seems younger than Criseyde, with a touch of the lovesick schoolboy in him. Sometimes also, as in these early scenes with Pandarus or the later bedroom scenes with Criseyde, their very different styles make Troilus's mannered speech and the romantic idealism it expresses seem a bit overblown and his character starts to verge on the comic.

That is what happens in Pandarus's long reply to the speech quoted above. Its avuncular,[4] slightly pompous, slightly pedantic tone quickly refocuses our image of the enamored Troilus:

> "Ye, Troilus, now herke," quod Pandare;
> "Though I be nyce, it happeth often so
> That oon that excesse doth ful yvele fare
> By good counseil kan kepe his frend therfro.
> I have myself ek seyn a blynd man goo
> There as he fel that couthe loken wyde:
> A fool may ek a wis-man ofte gide.
>
> A wheston is no kerving instrument,
> But yet it maketh sharppe kervyng tolis.
> And there thow woost that I have aught myswent,
> Eschuw thow that, for swich thing to the scole is;
> Thus often wise men ben war by foolys.
> If thou do so, thi wit is wel bewared;
> By his contrarie is every thyng declared."
>
> (I:624–37)

It is true that Troilus's gibe that Pandarus had never been a great success as a lover, and the pompous accumulation of platitudinous proverbs, turn the humor here back upon Pandarus himself. But at the same time, the fog of middle-aged common sense quickly chills the heat generated by Troilus's passion. And at the end of his long preachment, with Troilus still just lying there sighing, Pandarus nearly turns the scene into a farce, as he will do again in the consumation scene in Book III:

> [He] cryde "Awake!" ful wonderlich and sharpe:
> "What! slombrestow as in a litargie?
> Or artow like an asse to the harpe,
> That hereth sown whan men the strynges plye,
> But in his mynde of that no melodie
> May sinken him to gladen, for that he
> So dul is of his bestialite?"
>
> (I:729–35)

Late in the poem, the same contrast of Troilus's hyperbolic rhetoric with Pandarus's caustic common sense proves equally deflating but with less humor and considerably darker overtones. After it has been settled that Criseyde will be exchanged to the Greeks for Antenor, Troilus concludes his bitter "predestination soliloquy":

> Thanne seyde he thus: "Almyghty Jove in trone,
> That woost of al this thyng the sothfastnesse,
> Rewe on my sorow, and do me deyen sone,
> Or bryng Criseyde and me fro this destresse!"
> And whyl he was in al this hevynesse,
> Disputyng with himself in this matere,
> Com Pandare in, and seyde as ye may here.
>
> "O myghty God," quod Pandarus, "in trone,
> I! who say ever a wis man faren so?"
>
> (IV:1079–87)

A somewhat similar clashing of styles produces a quite different and considerably more ambiguous effect when Troilus's impassioned rhetoric encounters Criseyde's clear-eyed directness. In the bed-chamber scene at Pandarus's house, after Troilus, making passionate rhetoric rather than passionate love, has worked himself up to fainting in Criseyde's bed, he starts to recover from his swoon:

> And gan bet mynde and reson to hym take,
> But wonder soore he was abayst, iwis.
> And with a sik, whan he gan bet awake,
> He seyde "O mercy, God, what thyng is this?"
> "Why do ye with yourselven thus amys?"
> Quod tho Criseyde, "Is this a mannes game?
> What, Troilus, wol ye do thus for shame?"
>
> And therewithal hir arm over hym she leyde,
> And al foryaf, and ofte tyme hym keste.
>
> (III:1121–29)

It is possible to overemphasize the fact that Criseyde here must become the sexual aggressor, but her blunt "Is this a mannes game?" certainly forces us to raise some questions about Troilus's romantic idealism.

Chaucer achieves some of the subtlest and most skillful poetry in *Troilus and Criseyde* by this kind of offsetting of styles in scenes with Pandarus and Criseyde. It is tempting to quote long stretches of these charming, often witty, and wonderfully lifelike dialogues that, among other things, tell us so much about sophisticated medieval social intercourse. At times they remind us of Henry James in the way the surface language masks but at the same time half-reveals undercurrents of meaning of which the speakers themselves may be only partly conscious. Book II opens with one of the best such scenes, as Pandarus goes to Criseyde's house to begin his campaign to win her for Troilus:

> Whan he was come unto his neces place,
> "Wher is my lady?" to hire folk quod he;
> And they hym tolde, and he forth in gan pace,
> And fond two othere ladys sete, and she,
> Within a paved parlour, and they thre
> Herden a mayden reden hem the geste
> Of the siege of Thebes, while hem leste.
>
> Quod Pandarus, "Madame, God yow see,
> With al youre fayre book and compaignie!"
> "Ey, uncle myn, welcome iwys," quod she;
> And up she roos, and by the hond in hye
> She took him faste, and seyde, "This nyght thrie,
> To goode mot it turne, of yow I mette."
> And with that word she doun on bench hym sette.
>
> "Ye nece, yee shal faren wel the bet,
> If God wol, al this yeer," quod Pandarus;
> "But I am sory that I have yow let
> To herken of youre book ye preysen thus.
> For Goddess love, what seith it? telle it us!
> Is it of love? O, som good ye me leere!"
> "Uncle," quod she, "your maistresse is nat here."
>
> With that they gonnen laughe, and tho she seyde
> "This romaunce is of Thebes that we rede. . . ."
> (II:78–100)

Notice first that in this playful, bantering exchange the proverb-spouting and rather monitory tone of Pandarus's speeches to Troilus are gone. There is a certain Rotarian heavy-handedness about Pandarus's joking, but here both he and Criseyde are very civilized, quick-witted, sensitive people, and both are aware as they talk that their conversation is generating implications that are quite different from what they are literally saying.[5] That becomes clear several stanzas later, after Pandarus has worked the conversation around to a long and somewhat fulsome praise of Troilus, then starts to leave. Criseyde, sensing where he was trying to lead the conversation, yet not wanting to force the implications out into the open, quickly and with a gracious joke detains him and gives him the opportunity to come out with his real purpose:

> And with that word tho Pandarus, as blyve,
> He took his leve, and seyde, "I wol gon henne."
> "Nay, blame have I, myn uncle," quod she thenne.
>
> "What aileth yow to be thus wery soone,
> And namelich of wommen? Wol ye so?
> Nay, sitteth down; by God, I have to doone
> With yow, to speke of wisdom er ye go."
> And everi wight that was aboute hem tho,
> That herde that, gan fer away to stonde.
> Whil they two hadde al that hem liste in honde.
> (II:208–17)

Considerations of space prevent us from analyzing more examples of Chaucer's management of speech styles in these almost dramatic scenes. I hope that what has been shown in the notable examples discussed will suggest ways of reading that will enrich (and complicate) the reader's response to many other parts of the poem. But there is one more structural and stylistic strategy, different from what we have just been examining, but related to it, that we should consider quickly before turning to the perplexing conclusion of Chaucer's poem and the conclusion of this chapter about it.

At line 400 of Book I and again at line 638 of Book V, most of the surviving manuscripts of *Troilus and Criseyde* bear the rubric *Canticus Troili*. These two "songs of Troilus," set in a bit from the beginning and a little farther from the end, remind us of the lyrics Chaucer set into the *Book of the Duchess* and the *Parliament of Fowls* and the Prologue to the *Legend of Good Women*, although in *Troilus and Criseyde* he does not break the rhyme royal stanzaic pattern for them. They also mark the beginning and ending of a sequence of ten such "songs" in the poem, set pieces of varying lengths, all but two of them spoken by Troilus, where the action and any effective dramatic dialogue stop and we listen to technically elaborate lyric expressions. They could easily stand as separate poems in the manner of the French lyrics Chaucer imitated in most of his short poems.

In yet a different way, these lyric insets pull us back from the psychological empathy the dramatic dialogue scenes invite, now not to evoke either our tolerant amusement or our mature moral judgment, but rather our awareness of the eternal human passion at the heart of the poem, expressed in the Provençal and Petrarchan metaphors Chaucer had learned from his French and Italian exemplars to think of as the proper universal expression of that range of feeling. Specifically, these lyric inserts occur as follows:

Book I:400–434:	first *Canticus Troili*
Book II:827–75:	Antigone's song
Book III:1422:	Criseyde's *aubade*[6]
Book III:1450–70:	Troilus's answering *aubade*
Book III:1702–8:	Troilus's second *aubade*
Book III:1744–71:	Troilus's hymn to Love
Book IV:958–1082:	Troilus's predestination soliloquy
Book V:218–45:	Troilus's *complaint* "Wher is myn owene lady"
Book V:540–53:	Troilus's *complaint* to the empty palace
Book V:638–58:	second *Canticus Troili*

These passages are by no means all alike; they vary greatly in tone and style, as well as in the sources from which Chaucer adapted them. Two of them, Troilus's hymn to Love and his predestination soliloquy, even speak a metaphoric language that is distinctly Boethian rather than Provençal-Petrarchan, which certainly introduces yet another view of the love this poem is about.

We should probably look first and most carefully at the two Boethian passages, since much of the critical debate over the poem is about the moral and philosophical conflicts expressed in them. The first, Troilus's hymn to love at the end of Book III, is strategically placed at the center of the poem, at the height of Troilus's joy, just before catastrophe is to strike his great love:

> Love, that of erthe and se hath governaunce,
> Love, that his hestes hath in hevenes hye,
> Love, that with an holsom alliaunce

Halt peples joyned as hym lest hem gye,
Love, that knetteth lawe of compaignie,
And couples doth in vertu for to dwelle,
Bynd this acord, that I have told and telle.

That that the world with feith, which that is stable,
Diverseth so his stowndes concordynge,
That elementz that ben so discordable
Holden a bond perpetuely durynge,
That Phebus mote his rosy day forth brynge,
And that the mone hath lordshipe over the nyghtes,—
Al this doth Love, ay heried by his myghtes!

That that the se, that gredy is to flowen,
Constreyneth to a certeyn ende so
His flodes that so fiersly they ne growen
To drenchen erthe and al for evere mo;
And if that Love aughte lete his bridel go,
Al that now loveth asondre sholde lepe,
And lost were al that Love halt now to hepe.

So wolde God, that auctour is of kynde,
That with his bond Love of his vertu liste
To cerclen hertes alle, and faste bynde,
That from his bond no wight the wey out wiste;
And hertes colde, hem wolde I that he twiste
To make hem love, and that hem liste ay rewe
On hertes sore, and kepe hem that ben trewe!
(III:1744–71)

The song Chaucer has put in Troilus's mouth is based on a famous passage in Boethius's *Consolation of Philosophy,* in which Lady Philosophy tries to explain to Boethius how divine love governs the universe.

That the universe carries out its changing process in concord and with stable faith, that the conflicting seeds of things are held by everlasting law, that Phoebus in his golden chariot brings in the shining day, that the night, led by Hesperus, is ruled by Phoebe, that the greedy sea holds back his waves within lawful bounds, for they are not permitted to push back the unsettled earth—all this harmonious order of things is achieved by love which rules the earth and the seas, and commands the heavens.

But if love should slack the reins, all that is now joined in mutual love would wage continual war, and strive to tear apart the world which is now sustained in friendly concord by beautiful motion.

Love binds together people joined by a sacred bond; love binds sacred marriages by chaste affections; love makes the laws which join true friends. O how happy the human race would be, if that love which rules the heavens ruled also your souls.[7]

Troilus, of course, had no way of knowing he was paraphrasing an early Christian writer from several centuries after his own time, and it is probably just as well not to worry much over the anachronism of patently Christian phrases like "God, that auctour is of kynde" in the mouth of the Trojan prince. The point is that such Boethian language evokes in us a definition of love and order in terms of which Troilus's expression of the worth and importance of his passion for Criseyde seems at best very exaggerated. We must feel uneasy with the implication that this affair, however idealized, is somehow part of the Providential order in the universe. Something is out of scale, and our sense of it casts a faint shadow over Chaucer's otherwise blissful ending to Book III: "My thridde bok now ende ich in this wyse, / And Troilus in lust and in quiete / Is with Criseyde, his owen herte swete" (III:1818–20).

In the very next lines, the beginning of the proem to Book IV, the message Lady Philosophy had been trying to get through to Boethius about the impermanence of earthly things finds direct expression: "But al to litel, weylaway the whyle, / Lasteth such joie, ythonked be Fortune." As the mood of the poem darkens through Books IV and V, references to Fortune occur increasingly frequently, both by the narrator and by the charcaters in the poem. In a kind of ironic inversion of Boethius's resigned acceptance of the exigencies of Fortune, Pandarus and Troilus, particularly, repeatedly blame Fortune for the catastrophe as a way of unloading their own moral responsibility for the actions they had so joyfully participated in earlier. That shifting, sophistic moral deviousness is especially evident in Troilus's predestination soliloquy in IV:958–1082. The speech is too long to quote here in its entirety, but a few exerpts will show clearly what is going on. (Chaucer's principal source here is again Boethius, this time Book V, prose 2 and 3 of the *Consolation*).

"For al that comth, comth by necessitee:
Thus to ben lorn, it is my destinee.

For certeynly, this wot I wel" he seyde,
"That forsight of divine purveyaunce
Hath seyne alwey me to forgon Criseyde,
Syn God seeth every thyng out of doutaunce,
And hem disponyth, thorugh his ordinaunce,
In hire merites sothly for to be,
As they shul comen by predestyne."
(IV:958–66)

Again, let us pass over the anachronism and concentrate on the poetic effect. Troilus rightly perceives that there is a divine order in the universe, and that it works for purposes foreordained by God. The question of how God's absolute control of his own creation relates to the moral necessity for mortals to exercise free choice and judgment has troubled theologians from Boethius's time to our own. The deeper Troilus wiggles into its quicksands in this passage, the more confused he becomes, and the moral judgments become correspondingly more difficult for us:

But natheles, allas! whom shal I leeve?
For ther ben grete clerkes many oon,
That destyne thorugh argumentes preve;
And som men seyn that nedely, ther is noon,
But that fre chois is yeven us everychon.
(IV:967–71)

In the end, the best Troilus can do to reconcile his great love, its loss, the arbitrariness of Fortune, and the will of God is to despair of further action on his own and indirectly absolve himself of responsibility for what has happened:

Thus in this same wise, out of doutance,
I may wel maken, as it semeth me,
My resonyng of Goddes purveyaunce
And of the thynges that to comen be;
By which resoun men may wel yse
That thilke thynges that in erthe falle,
That by necessite they comen alle.
(IV:1044–50)

The other eight of the lyriclike inserts, however, rarely echo these Boethian undertones and pull us emotionally in rather different directions. The two *Cantici Troili* derive from Petrarch and Boccaccio, respectively, and their metaphoric language is the conventional paradoxical expression of the simultaneous joy and pain, hope and despair, of idealized sexual passion. Antigone's song is a pastiche of the French lyrics so important to Chaucer's dream poems, and the three *aubades* and two *complaints* belong solidly to the same tradition.

What these songs do for us finally, besides adding much to the beautiful music of the poem, is to define the ideal love Troilus was seeking and thought he had found. But they also define it, and this is of the greatest importance, not just as his own self-destructive illusion. That it is expressed in these conventional forms reminds us that Troilus is sharing a frequently expressed, very widespread if not universal, human experience. Because Criseyde's experience of the same relationship is quite different, and the narrator's and Pandarus's and our views of it different still, we must also see the serious limitations and dangers in Troilus's kind of love, which, however, partly because of these lyric passages, Chaucer's poem demands that we understand and take seriously.

The ending of *Troilus and Criseyde,* that is, what follows after Pandarus's superbly apt curtain line "I kan namore seye" at line 1743, has been a source of endless debate about what conclusions Chaucer finally wanted us to reach about his finished love story. Two different groups of surviving manuscripts have quite different versions of the ending of Book V and of several earlier parts of the poem, and many modern editors follow Root[8] in concluding that Chaucer made at least one and possibly two revisions of the poem. Some eminent critics, most notably C. S. Lewis,[9] have felt that the ending, whether added in a revision or not, was an artistic mistake that cannot be made to square with the rest of the poem.

However it got that way, I think it must be said that there is a troubling awkwardness, a too obvious creaking of rhetorical machinery, in the poem's last hundred or so lines, that adds to our discomfort with the overt, flat-footed Christian moralizing upon the wonderfully subtle and complex poem we have just read. The awkwardness does not show up at once. After Pandarus's memorable exit line, Chaucer (in a manner we have by now become used to) backs away from the dramatic immediacy of the scene for one last time and the whole story recedes once more into the old books from which he took it. From lines 1765 to 1798, the narrator goes through the standard rhetorical motions for closing a poem: a reminder of his purpose in writing and of sources we can go to if we want to pursue the story further, an appeal to his readers for their tolerance and goodwill, and finally the envoy addressed to his own book as, having folded these vital lively and loving characters back into its pages, he puts it up on the shelf beside the others. If nothing of the poem after line 1798 of Book V had survived, I suspect no one would ever have supposed there was to have been anything more to the poem—except that the last stanza would be lacking its final line.

But the rest of the poem is there and we have no reason to think Chaucer did not write it. The last line of the stanza that could have concluded the poem so naturally is "But yet to purpose of my rather speche" (now to get back to what I was talking about). From there on, we get a series of unexpected jolts. First, we see Troilus, after he is killed in battle by Achilles, ascending to a kind of heaven in the eighth sphere. We are given no hint of how he deserved such a transformation or what power was responsible for sending him there. And the Troilus we see is extremely hard to identify with the passionate, idealistic young man we had come to know in the preceding five books:

> And in hymself he lough right at the wo
> Of hem that wepten for his deth so faste;
> And dampned al oure werk that foloweth so
> the blynde lust, the which that may nat laste,
> And sholden al oure herte on hevene caste.
> V:1821–25)

Troilus is at last able to look at himself and his love objectively, as he had never been able to do when alive, but it is from such a distance—the ultimate distance, from the other side of death—that all humanity is gone from him and what he sees. Although that may be the way human affairs look from eternity, it is not the way they feel to living readers and living Chaucerian characters.

Something of that is implied, I think, in the much more humane apostrophe Chaucer addresses to the "yonge, fresshe folkes" at line 1835:

> O yonge, fresshe folkes, he or she,
> In which that love up groweth with youre age,

> Repeyreth hom fro worldly vanyte,
> And of youre herte up casteth the visage
> To thilke God that after his ymage
> Yow made, and thynketh al nys but a faire
> This world, that passeth soone as floures faire.
> (V:1835–41)

For all their reassertion of its transitoriness, these lines still reflect accurately the beauty and the inevitability ("In which that love up groweth with youre age") of the human experience of young love.

Chaucer did not, after all, simply destroy all the earlier parts of his poem once he had set forth Troilus's disembodied view from the eighth sphere. All five books are still there, in all their complexity and ambiguity, and the poem's various and conflicting senses of what was happening, its painful and comic admixture of sympathetic understanding and objective judgment. Even after the dedication to the "moral Gower" and the "Philosophical Strode" and the solemn Dantean prayer of the concluding stanza, what we take away from this poem is our complicated image of the flawed and transitory but great love of Troilus and Criseyde.

Chapter Seven
Canterbury Tales

The last of Chaucer's great projects, which, typically, he left unfinished, is the one that most of us associate first with his name, although readers in earlier times did not automatically do so. It is true that one of the first English books William Caxton chose to print on his imported press in 1478, the first printing press in England, was an edition of the *Canterbury Tales,* followed by a second edition, based on a different manuscript, in 1483. But until past the middle of the seventeenth century, it was the dream poems and *Troilus and Criseyde* that attracted most of Chaucer's admirers and imitators. That probably tells us more about the history of taste than it does about the quality of Chaucer's poetry. John Dryden, in the late seventeenth century, and his eighteenth- and nineteenth-century successors, became increasingly interested in literature that represented first a kind of realistic typology of human behavior and then the psychological realism of emotional representation. Until well into the twentieth century, that fascination with the glimpses of medieval or universal reality that we catch in the fragments of this great uncompleted ruin of a poem has dominated the general appreciation of Chaucer's work.

The response is not at all unwarranted. But it is a highly selective response, one that takes into account only parts of what we have of the *Canterbury Tales* and rarely faces up to the enormous problems we are left with by the state in which the surviving manuscripts of the poem have come down to us. So again we have to begin with the problems rather than the pleasures, but especially in the case of the *Canterbury Tales,* that approach has its virtues. We simply cannot read that poem without knowing how its text came to us, and we must finally read all of what we can make out of that scrambled textual transmission to be what Chaucer had written when he left the leaves of unfinished manuscript on his desk in October 1400.

No manuscript of the *Canterbury Tales* survives that Chaucer could possibly have seen. All are copies made by fifteenth-century scribes, many of whom felt obligated to edit and improve the texts they copied. None of these extant copies can be dated earlier than 1410, more than ten years after Chaucer's death. Between about 1410 and 1478 (the date of Caxton's first printed edition), we now know of eighty-four such manuscript copies, many of them incomplete and some only very small fragments. By the way, this is a fairly large number of surviving manuscripts for a medieval work,[1] and it may imply that the *Canterbury Tales* enjoyed a greater popularity among its general fifteenth-century readership than it did with the poets and critics.

As we might expect under such circumstances, there is a wide variation among the versions presented by the various manuscripts, so that editors ever since Caxton have had to wrestle with the enormous problem of which version to prefer, or where and how to combine the seemingly preferable parts of different versions. Particularly since about the middle of the nineteenth century, when some of the manuscripts came to light and new and better techniques for analyzing them developed, large amounts of the scholarly attention and energy devoted to Chaucer's poetry have gone into trying to establish a standard text, but there is still no universal agreement. Any printed text of the *Canterbury Tales* a reader picks up represents of necessity a host of decisions the editor has had to make about which manuscript to use as a base and where and how to improve it by using readings from other manuscripts or correcting what that particular editor thinks are mistakes in one or another manuscript. Since it is highly unlikely that all editors will ever agree about all such decisions, we shall just have to live with the present situation, using various editions by intelligent, well-informed, careful scholars presenting various versions of the text.

For the beginning reader, many of those variations will not matter much. But many of them do matter a great deal, and I will discuss some of the major ones here, partly so that no one will assume that the particular text he reads is assuredly just what Chaucer wrote, but mainly so that we will always keep in mind what even seasoned scholar-critics may sometimes forget, that we are dealing with an unfinished poem, the exact text of which we can never be absolutely certain about. For this reason, some important critical questions about the *Canterbury Tales* simply cannot be answered or must be answered only tentatively and with heavy qualifications.

There are in general two kinds of textual variation among the surviving manuscripts, the first more amenable to scholarly resolution than the second. If one sat down, as careful editors do, and just read through all eighty-four of the manuscripts, or better still, arranged them side by side so that each line could be compared, the first kind of variation would quickly become apparent: thousands of differences in spelling and wording, omissions or transpositions of phrases or lines—that is, relatively mechanical variations, many of which modern linguistic and orthographic knowledge and careful attention to what makes sense in Chaucer's sentences can resolve relatively easily. There are not many real differences among good modern texts on these matters, although some notable cruxes remain to be argued over. However, the footnotes in a good edition always point these out, so again the beginning reader need not worry much about them.

The second type of manuscript variation is much more noticeable and important, not only as a factor in the differences among modern editions, but also as an indication of the state in which Chaucer left his poem at his death and how much editorial arranging and rearranging fifteenth-century scribes must have done as they copied it. It will be easier to get at this problem if we leave the surviving manuscripts for a moment to consider what we can recover of Chaucer's own plan for the poem.

Near the end of the General Prologue, Harry Bailly, the host of the Tabard Inn, attaches himself to the party of pilgrims, takes over as its unofficial master of ceremonies, and gets the pilgrims to agree to a plan for amusing themselves along the way to Canterbury:

> This is the poynt, to speken short and pleyn,
> That ech of yow, to shorte with oure weye,
> In this viage shal telle tales tweye
> To Caunterbury-ward, I mene it so,
> And homward he shal tellen othere two,
> Of aventures that whilom han bifalle.
> (I:790–95)

Chaucer had informed us earlier that the pilgrims were "wel nyne and twenty in a compaignye," presumably including himself, but not the Host, who had not yet joined the group. The narrator's account of the group in the Tabard the night before the pilgrimage begins is in fact vague in many of its details, so that it is hard to pin down the exact number of pilgrims. Furthermore, late in the work as we now have it, two unexpected travellers overtake them and one of these, the

Canon's Yeoman, tells a tale. So it is clear that Chaucer never finally settled even the exact number of pilgrims he intended to appear. But some revealing comparisons can be made without mathematical exactness, and we will use thirty as a fairly close round figure. The Host's scheme, then, should provide in the finished poem 120 tales, four by each pilgrim. A good deal later, along the road to Canterbury, one of the Host's remarks seems to imply, though not at all clearly, that Chaucer may have changed his plan to one tale each way from each pilgrim, which would have resulted in a total of sixty. What we actually have of the poem includes twenty-three tales, one of them (the Squire's) unfinished, and a bare beginning of a twenty-fourth, the Cook's. We have no good reason to suppose Chaucer wrote any more.

Our difficulty is not just that Chaucer finished only a little more than a third of what even the minimum plan would have called for. Just before the Host appears and takes over management of the pilgrimage, the narrator tells us

> But now is tyme to yow for to telle
> How that we baren us that ilke nyght,
> Whan we were in that hostelrie alyght;
> And after wol I telle of oure viage
> And al the remenaunt of oure pilgrimage.
> (I:720–24)

The finished poem, then, had it ever been written, would have had a complete account of the journey from Southwark to Canterbury and back, framing the tales and linking them together with descriptions of the route and landscape and a record of the conversation and interaction among the travelers between tales. As it turned out, Chaucer's frame story of "our viage" never gets the pilgrims to Canterbury. And he wrote what he did complete of the frame narrative in bits and pieces, so that only small groups of tales are actually connected by linking narrative. The result is ten fragments, two of only one tale (that is, one with no framing narrative to link it to a preceding or following one) and the longest fragment consisting of six tales.

Let us now return to the variant manuscripts and the question of the order in which to arrange these fragments. We know, of course, as did all the fifteenth-century scribal editors, that Fragment I begins the poem, starting with the General Prologue, and the continuing narrative leads directly into the Knight's Tale, followed by continuing accounts of interaction among the pilgrims between tales, unmistakably linking the Miller's Tale with the Knight's, the Reeve's with the Miller's, and the beginning of the Cook's with the Reeve's. However, when the Cook's Tale breaks off after 57 lines, there is simply no way to know which fragment should come next. For reasons that may not be absolutely compelling, most editors, including the fifteenth-century scribes, have assumed that Fragment X, the Parson's Tale and Chaucer's "Retraction," concludes the poem. Thus we have fixed places for Fragments I and X, but as far as any controlling evidence from the frame story is concerned, the eight fragments between could be placed in any order.

It is not the case that the surviving manuscripts offer us every possible different arrangement of those eight fragments, but there are importantly different orders in different manuscripts. To the extent that we assume Chaucer meant the *Canterbury Tales* to be a coherent whole poem, we have to be concerned with its structure, the order and interrelation of its parts; therefore, modern editors remain much concerned with establishing an order for the fragments and are not fully agreed on what it should be.

To illustrate the difficulty briefly, F. N. Robinson's edition, which I have been using throughout this study, prints the fragments in the order in which they appear in what he and many other modern scholars consider the best of the fifteenth-century manuscripts, the Ellesmere Manuscript, and numbers them in order with Roman numerals I through X. But in the nineteenth century scholars noticed that if the fragments are arranged that way, some of the references in the frame story to places the pilgrims passed on the road are out of order. Curiously, in no surviving manuscript is there a sequence of fragments that does keep the geography straight, though the place references are rather scant in any case, and Chaucer himself may have rearranged some of the tales without getting around to the revisions that would straighten out the place references. After a good deal of pioneering textual work, the Chaucer Society, in its *Six-Text Edition of the Canterbury Tales,* edited by Walter W. Skeat, published in 1911 an arrangement attempting to sort out the geography. This arrangement (if we keep Robinson's numbering for the sake of comparison) orders the fragments I, II, VII, VI, III, IV, V, VIII, IX, X. Robert A. Pratt followed that order, with some modification, in his recent edition.[2]

In the end, even though the order in which we read its parts is of first importance to the effect any long poem has on us, we just have to leave the matter of the order of the *Canterbury Tales* up in the air. So let us try to remember always as readers that we are working with fragments of an unfinished poem, already under revision at the time of Chaucer's death, and which have been transmitted to us by intermediaries of uncertain reliability.

What, then, is left for us to make of these fragments? A very great deal indeed. Modern scholarship has provided us with texts far more reliable than anything Dryden, Spenser, or Shakespeare had. And giving full allowance for the critical precautions I have been urging, those ten fragments contain some of the best poetry in our language. No one, I suspect, has ever read them attentively without feeling intuitively that they do belong together, that complex themes start to develop in them, that there are intimations of fascinating interrelationships among characters and tales, and that we can often hear at its poetically most effective that characteristically Chaucerian divergent polyphony of voices.

The first fragment, beginning with the General Prologue, is an obvious starting place. It seems surely a polished, finished piece, making us feel that this is what the whole poem would have been like had Chaucer completed it. And it introduces that memorable cast of pilgrim characters that from the beginning has been a major attraction for readers. I will argue later that we can go wrong by weighting too heavily these characterizations in our overall view of the poem, but Chaucer obviously expended great care on them. The delightful colored portraits of the pilgrims that decorate the margins of the Ellesmere Manuscript are a sure indication that already in the early fifteenth century readers and manuscript illuminators were responding to the lifelikeness of these characters and visualizing them. These protraits of the pilgrims, all of them properly on horseback, are painted in at the beginning of each pilgrim's tale, but whoever made them had obviously read Chaucer's descriptions of them in the General Prologue and made each picture closely correspond to the word-portrait.[3]

The character to be considered first is the pilgrim narrator who, although we cannot be absolutely sure, may be known to the Man of Law and some of the other pilgrims as Geoffrey Chaucer. It is his voice we hear at the opening of the poem, although for the first eighteen lines it remains detached and impersonal, masked by the elaborate rhetoric that plants the clues we are to follow in reading this pilgrimage as both literal and metaphoric, particular and universal. Then, at line twenty, much in the manner of the narrators of the dream poems, this voice starts to become embodied as a character in the fiction, yet one still sufficiently apart from it to talk to us about it. Characteristically, he never supplies us with a portrait of himself, although much later, in Fragment VII, Harry Bailly gives us an abbreviated one as he invites the narrator-pilgrim to take his turn in the tale telling:

> "What man artow," quod he;
> "Thou lookest as thou woldest fynde an hare,
> For evere upon the ground I se thee stare.
>
> Approche neer, and looke up murily.
> Now war yow, sires, and lat this man have place!
> He in the waast is shape as wel as I;
> This were a popet in an arm t'embrace
> For any woman, smal and fair of face.
> He semeth elvyssh by his contenaunce,
> For unto no wight dooth he daliaunce."
>
> (VII:695–704)

Chaucer may never have wanted us to visualize him, but only to listen to him, partly as the creator of this marvelous poetry, partly as an accurate recorder of what he heard his fellow pilgrims and other writers saying, partly as a participant projected by his own imagination into the action his fiction creates.

The opening lines of the General Prologue and then the series of portraits of the pilgrims have, ever since Dryden's time, received so much critical attention and interpretative commentary that it seems difficult and superfluous to start afresh on them here. The bibliography at the end of this volume provides a general guide to the many available commentaries. However, although it is not an entirely original idea, I should like to discuss here the new version this opening fragment, and subsequent ones as well, gives us of the multiple and ambivalent narrative voices we have been observing in the earlier poems.

For the first eighteen lines, we hear a voice almost like those great "auctoritees" Chaucer was always sending us to in the dream poems and *Troilus and Criseyde,* a voice that speaks easily in the high style, laying out in a single, complex eighteen-line sentence a combination of nature description, zodiacal metaphor, classical allusion, and local reference that makes it clear we are to attend to this poem in several different ways at once. Its narrator announces himself capable of telling us about not only the pilgrimage his little group will make from London to Canterbury, but also the metaphorically equivalent pilgrimages the seasons and the planets make through their cyclical rounds. The successive classical and then Christian allusions probably also imply something about yet another medieval meaning of "pilgrimage," all humanity's pilgrimage from creation through time toward eternity.

Especially in the General Prologue, the arbitrary and unrealistic, yet utterly convincing, shifts in the narrator's perspective keep us aware of the different but somehow coherent meanings of his story. At line 20, he drops us abruptly into an almost Dickensian first person; surely now the fiction is about to become all-encompassing, the narrator a character in it, and we will lose ourselves in a fascinating re-creation of fourteenth-century life. But almost at once the pseudorealism goes askew. Our humble pilgrim sitting at the back table in Harry Bailly's bar knows and tells us things about these pilgrims that he could never have observed from there, very much as the more impersonal voice of the opening lines had spoken from some unknown location outside the cyclical events it was reporting.

This is not a matter of whether something is wrong with Chaucer's "realism," but rather of what his General Prologue begins to suggest. The fictive narrator could never have known from his Southwark tavern bench how the Knight was dressed when he got off the boat to start his pilgrimage, or what kind of horse the Shipman rode and how skilled a moonlight navigator he was. The main point is not even that the narrator wants us to know those things; it is, again, that we follow his clues and learn to look at things in more than one way at a time. We not only imagine our way into the midst of lively fourteenth-century tavern life; we also attend to a poem being made about it, a poem that will show us several kinds of meaning besides the historical and representational.

Many of the portraits of the pilgrims in the General Prologue involve us in some kind of divergence of perspective. There are in this group no saints, with the possible exception of the Parson, and no absolutely lost souls, with the possible exception of the Pardoner.

What the narrator, in his uncensuring innocence, offers us most of the time are characterizations upon which he refuses to make any overt judgments, but which we can usually evaluate in at least two different ways. Is the Knight a nearly perfect idealistic Christian soldier or a skilled professional mercenary? He is the highest of the pilgrims in social rank, and perhaps in consequence, Chaucer describes him first. The opening lines of the description are unambiguous, unqualified praise:

> A knyght ther was, and that a worthy man,
> That fro the tyme that he first bigan
> To riden out, he loved chivalrie,
> Trouthe and honour, fredom and curteisie.
> (I:43–46)

And in addition to his secular virtues of "trouthe and honour, fredom and curteisie"—the conventional virtues of the storybook hero knights of the romances—most of his military career had been spent in crusading holy wars. But we may begin to feel a little uneasy a few lines later when we are told that

> This ilke worthy knyght hadde been also
> Sometyme with the lord of Palatye
> Agayn another hethen in Turkye.
> And everemoore he hadde a sovereyn prys. . . .
> (I:64–67)

Those lines seem to tell us that, for a good enough price, he could be bought as a hired sword by the very Mohammedans he had spent much of his life crusading against. Indeed, some modern critics have argued that such elements in his description should cause us to see him as a hypocritical soldier of fortune who most of the time can cloak his love of the bloody game of warfare in the high-sounding covers of "chivalry" and "crusading." It is surely wrongheaded for us to try to reduce to only one the multiple impressions Chaucer carefully evokes.

To turn from this plain, hardy old field soldier to the portrait that follows of his permanented and perfumed son, the Squire, is to sharpen even further our awareness of how many levels of meaning Chaucer is operating on. Like his father, the Knight, the Squire is a character out of the romances. But the marvelous irony is that he typifies just what the old ideal chivalry was actually becoming in Chaucer's time, and would continue to be down to Shakespeare's: a kind of playacting in aristocratic tournament fields in gorgeous costume-armor. So the "reality" of chivalry is that it is becoming a deliberate fiction, while the Knight's stubborn attempts to realize the chivalric ideals increasingly relegate him to a lost fictional world of the past. That is not merely a generation gap, but a whole cultural fault line. Only the greatest poetry can compress into a few dozen lines that kind of revealing insight.

But that is far from all; the Squire may be much more than we infer from his curly hair and modish embroidered tunic, with its sleeves cut in the newest French fashion. He is an excellent athlete—"wonderly delyvere and of greet strengthe"—and has already had a commendable apprenticeship in the field in France. Although his father probably would have viewed such accomplishments less favorably than we do, the Squire was also an excellent dancer, something of a poet, and a sketcher, and he could even read and write. But the touch Chaucer reserves for the last in his portrait is perhaps most meaningful. Despite the generation gap, the Squire understands, respects, and honors his father: "Curteis he was, lowely, and servysable, / And carf biforn his fader at the table."

Eighteen lines later, the portrait of the Prioress offers us an even subtler mixture of perspectives—subtler because she is in religious orders. However much we know that those in holy orders are nonetheless human beings, whenever we become particularly aware of their humanity, it seems inevitably to be a kind of lapse from their vocation. Is the Prioress a sentimental, vain, worldly woman, or a tenderhearted religious trying to do everything as beautifully as possible in the service of the Lord? Or is she the former, trying hard and sometimes successfully to be the latter?

Chaucer rather stacks the deck against her in the opening lines by telling us first about her coy smile and her genteel swearing, and that she is named Eglentyne, after the conventional clinging vine heroine of several medieval romances. But she is by no means the character out of a Tennessee Williams play those early lines alone would make her seem. She *is* a prioress—the head and administrator of her convent—whose careful French was surely an asset to her and her convent in the bilingual society she had to deal with. And Chaucer tells us

At mete wel ytaughte was she with alle;
She leet no morsel from hir lippes fallt,
Ne wette hir fingres in hir sauce depe;
Wel koude she carie a morsel and wel kepe
That no drope ne fille upon hir brest.
(I: 127–31)

We may well share the amusement of many of Chaucer's contemporaries at recognizing her table manners as identical with those taught to an aspiring young courtesan by an old whore in the *Roman de la rose.* We ought, equally, to ask ourselves the other question: how would her service to her office and her order be improved by clumsy table behavior and a gravy-spattered wimple? Where does personal vanity end and respect for her position in her order and in society begin, and how far can they overlap? That conflict is raised to an exquisite tension in the description of her rosary that concludes her portrait:

Of smal coral aboute hire arm she bar
A peire of bedes, gauded al with grene,
And theron heng a brooch of gold ful sheene,
On which ther was first write a crowned A,
And after *Amor vincit omnia.*
(I: 158–62)

In the deepest sense of the Prioress's religious vocation, love must indeed conquer all, and her prayer beads are the symbols of her expression of the divine love that has conquered her. But we also see that rosary as a gorgeous piece of jewelry worn by a beautiful woman, and many of us (like most of Chaucer's first readers) will recall the elegantly carved ivory mirror backs on the cosmetic tables of fourteenth-century belles, with their cupids and amorous couples and the motto—carved around the circumference—*amor vincit omnia.* Chaucer almost nags us with that painful ambiguity by repeating it, in the next portrait, of the Monk who fastened his hood with a "curious pyn" of gold with "A love knotte in the gretter ende."

In several of the other portraits the multiple impressions involve different conflicts and ambiguities. In some, like the Friar and the Shipman and the Miller, obvious rascals are given such lively abilities and/or personality traits that we grudgingly admire them even as we recognize their roguery. Still others, like the Clerk and the Parson, are obviously good sober men who just verge on lacking enough human warmth and vitality to engage our sympathy. In still other cases, Chaucer will create an unmistakable double entendre and leave it to us to juggle the two different readings. How do we read "worthy" when the narrator tells us the Friar was "familiar" with "worthy wommen of the toun?" Or when he tells us Alice of Bath "was a worthy womman al hir lyve?" When we are told of the Merchant, "Their wiste no wight that he was in dette," do we conclude that he was in debt but was careful to keep anyone from knowing about it, or that there was no evidence that he owed anyone anything? Even to phrase the questions as I have just done points the wrong way. No amount of critical debate will settle these "either-or" questions, because the portraits clearly suggest both. That is partly Chaucer's "realism," his representation of characters who appear to us as mixed, as ambiguous, in motive and action, as people in real life do. But it is partly also a subtle comic indication that these are "fallen" men and women whose pilgrimage toward eternity will, because of the fall, inevitably be motivated by an indistinguishable mixture of the spirit and the flesh. Since our narrator is, in this fiction, one of them also, the same applies to him.

It is a major frustration of the *Canterbury Tales* that its unfinished, fragmentary state will not permit us to follow out these suggestions, which seem so provocative in the General Prologue. At the end of it, as these set portraits dissolve into dialogue and dramatic action and the travelers start along the Canterbury road, we look forward to a fictional enactment of the human and thematic potential of the portraits. And this is what we find throughout the rest of the first fragment. There is not only the social and psychological contrast between the Knight and the Miller and the Reeve; the courtly idealism of the Knight's Tale is set off by the cheerful sexual realism of the Miller's Tale and the sourer, harsher cheating and finagling in the Reeve's Tale. A wonderful narrative complexity is beginning to develop. The dramatic interaction among these three characters has social and ethical implications as well as psychological ones. The three tales, different as they are, do have clear thematic links. All three seem to most of us like the kind of stories we would expect such men to tell. That is, they seem to add to our impressions of the tellers, as well as develop their own narrative characteristics.

The Knight, highest ranking of the pilgrims on the medieval social scale, draws the straw that makes him also the teller of the first tale. His first of the *Canterbury Tales* is a long, serious, romantic, philosophical poem that at times seems near the verge of ironic comedy. In some ways it is what we might expect from an idealistic medieval knight, although we know that Chaucer had been working on different versions of the story much earlier in his career. Its central plot is a typical medieval love story: two young noblemen fall in love with the same woman, at first hopelessly, and then after a series of miraculous coincidences, do battle for her hand. Yet the tale is really as much about preserving a civilized order in a chaotic and violent world as it is about the lovers. The tale is filled with the pageantry of elaborate rituals for the containment of violent passions: the codes of warfare; the etiquette of love rivalry; the rules of the medieval tournament; and the funeral ceremony. What we see in it mainly is an ideal of noble conduct—paradoxically, even the civilized conduct of conflict and hostility. Near the end of the tale, Duke Theseus (anachronistically borrowing his metaphor from Boethius) gives us a long definition of that notion of civilized order:

> The Firste Moevere of the cause above
> Whan he first made the faire cheyne of love,
> Greet was th'effect, and heigh was his entente.
> Wel wiste he why, and what thereof he mente;
> For with that faire cheyne of love he bond
> The fyr, the eyr, the water, and the lond
> In certeyn boundes, that they may nat flee.
> That same Prince and the Moevere," quod he,
> "Hath stablissed in this wrecched world adoun
> Certeyne dayes and duracioun
> To al that is engendred in this place,
> Over the whiche day they may nat pace,
> Al mowe they yet tho dayes wel abregge."
> (I:2987–99)

For Theseus, a loving God firmly ruling an ordered universe is the model for his conduct of the affairs of his own dukedom. Whatever is done, including living, fighting, and dying, is to be done properly and by the rules.

When the Knight has finished his tale, the Host compliments him and asks the Monk to tell the next tale. But Harry Bailly is no Theseus; the drunken Miller loudly asserts himself, shattering the order of precedence and authority the Host was trying to maintain:

> The Millere, that for dronken was al pale
> So that unnethe upon his horse he sat,
> He nolde avalen neither hood ne hat,
> Ne abyde no man for his curteisie,
> But in Pilates voys he gan to crie,
> And swoor, "By armes, and by blood and bones,
> I kan a noble tale for the nones,
> With which I wol now quite the Knyghtes tale."
> (I:3120–27)

The Miller's interruption opens up the plan of the *Canterbury Tales* to all manner of unpredictable interruptions and diversions; it also introduces a theme that will recur in various ways. When he says his tale will "quite" the Knight's, that is, answer back to it or get even with it, he is not only unknowingly foreshadowing the Reeve's angry attempt to "quit" the Miller and his tale; he is also beginning a pattern of answering back and getting even that underlies several pairs of tales and their tellers: the Knight and the Miller, the Reeve and the Miller, the Friar and the Summoner, the Clerk and the Wife of Bath, and in a brief but violent exchange, the Host and the Pardoner.

It is probably better not to ask whether a drunken Miller would be capable of the complex subtlety with which the Miller's Tale "quits" the Knight's. It is, nevertheless, a nice parodic inversion of the main themes of the Knight's Tale. Its main plot concerns two young men competing for the same woman. Alisoun, however, is no duke's daughter, but a country wench; and although Nicholas, the Oxford man, can speak the language of the noble love of Palamon and Arcite for Emily, he and Absolon operate on a social level far below that of Theseus's court. And their "duel" is fought out in a place and manner and with "weapons" that are the opposite of chivalric. Again, there is in the Miller's Tale much ordering and arranging of things, but none of it is directed to preserving the dignity and containing the passions of the noble life. The way the natural order of things asserts itself at the end of the tale is closer to Laurel and Hardy than it is to Boethius.

Still, underneath the slapstick sexual comedy, a kind of order of things *is* working—a rough poetic justice in which everyone finally gets pretty much what he deserved, as the Miller bluntly sums it up in his conclusion:

> Thus swyved was this carpenteris wyf,
> For al his kepyng and his jalousye;
> And Absolon hath kist hir nether yë;
> And Nicholas is scalded in the towte.
> This tale is doon, and God save al the rowte!
> (I:3850–54)

As Robin the Miller's ale-roughened voice ceases, our pilgrim-narrator deftly leads us back into one of those rapid, sharp-edged dramatic dialogues that compel us to try to imagine what we might have had if Chaucer had completed all of his frame story:

> Whan folk hadde laughen at this nyce cas
> Of Absolon and hende Nicholas,
> Diverse folk diversely they seyde,
> But for the moore part they loughe and pleyde.
> Ne at this tale I saugh no man him greve,
> But it were oonly Osewold the Reve.
> (I:3855–60)

We have already been told in the General Prologue that Oswald the Reeve is a sour, vengeful, deceitful man, but his angry response to the Miller's Tale here leads into a different version of "quitting"—tale answering back to tale, and one teller getting even with (or one up on) another. The Knight and the Miller are more or less at opposite ends of the social spectrum represented in the Canterbury pilgrims. Still, the Miller's "quitting" of the Knight is neither personal nor socially invidious. He seems rather to be saying "look, Sir Romantically Deluded Knight, here's how love triangles *really* work." It is debatable how much the Reeve is above the Miller socially, but Oswald, like many newly risen on the social ladder, is very thin-skinned about his former trade as a carpenter and very stiff-necked about his status as a kind of business manager on a feudal manor. So the primary motives for his "quitting" of the Miller are reflected in the class jealousies and mean-spirited revenges of the tale he tells. Probably that is not exactly what Oswald meant to do; his angry intent is to show a vicious miller getting what is coming to him, because the Reeve took the Miller's Tale of a cuckolded carpenter to be a personal affront to all carpenters or ex-carpenters. But both in his own character and in the way his tale reflects it, we have not only a "quitting" of the Miller, but an indirect response to the Knight's Tale. Compare the concern of nearly everyone in the Knight's Tale for stability, order, and a proper and fixed precedence of authority, with the spiteful, distrustful scratching and clawing for a leg up on the social or economic ladder in the Reeve's Tale.

So the third tale of the first fragment, along with its link to the second, continues to reinforce the intuition that a very large and complex poetic intention underlies the *Canterbury Tales.* The three tales, and their tellers, are very different from each other; nevertheless, several psychological, social, and moral—and even religious—issues are beginning to take shape.

Even as the Reeve is finishing his tale with "Thus have I quyt the Millere in my tale," the cook is slapping him on the back and promising, not to "quit" him, but to keep the string of dirty stories going. And this time the Host doesn't even try to redirect the game of storytelling that has already gotten quite out of his control. Instead, he gets in a little advance "quitting" of his own, needling cook Roger of Ware for his sloppy, unsanitary, and deceitful cookery. But this time it seems to be all in good humor, and Hodge the cook (quite unlike Oswald the reeve) replies in the same light-hearted vein:

> And therfore, Herry Bailly, by thy feith,
> Be thou nat wrooth, er we departen heer,
> Though that my tale be of an hostileer.
> But natheless I wol nat tell it yit;
> But er we parte, ywis, thou shalt be quit.
> (I:4358–62)

Although the beginning of the Cook's tale looks suspiciously like another fabliau, we get only the first 57 lines of it, and we never get a chance to hear how a cook's "quitting" of a social-climbing bartender might continue to develop the patterns we have been noting. After Fragment I breaks off, we will encounter this kind of fully realized complexity only here and there among the other fragments.

Apparently, however, few readers have ever left the *Canterbury Tales* without feeling that various groups of tales are somehow linked together thematically or stylistically, even though the actual manuscript groupings may not so arrange them. One of the most widely known (and earlier in the twentieth century, most hotly debated) of such groupings was Kittredge's suggestion of a "marriage group," starting with the Wife of Bath's Tale and continuing through Fragments III, IV, and V, concluding with the Franklin's Tale, which Kittredge read as an expression of the ideal solution to the problem of sovereignty in marriage first raised by the Wife of Bath.[4] Some subsequent critics, especially those who follow the order of some of the manuscripts mentioned above and put Fragment VII after Fragment II, would thus have the "marriage group" start with the Shipman's Tale, even before we get to the Wife of Bath. Such are the problems left us by the discrepancies among the manuscripts.

But it is by no means simply a textual problem. Kittredge's suggestion of a "marriage group" implies a notion of design, of blocks of tales dealing with specific themes, and that is not at all the same thing as noticing that the subject of marriage comes up in various tales scattered throughout the work. The tales of the Knight, Miller, Reeve, and Man of Law are also concerned in various ways with love and marriage, as in truth are more than half of the tales. Even in the group as Kittredge first suggested it, there are difficulties. Fragments III, IV, and V (and remember, there are no links between fragments; we know only that most manuscripts put them in that order) consist of the tales of the Wife of Bath, the Friar, and the Summoner; the Clerk and the Merchant; and the Squire and the Franklin. The tales of the Friar and Summoner have nothing to do with marriage, and are instead a further round of "quitting" between the two rogues. And the Squire's Tale, though it is clearly some sort of romance, with a love story at its center, is unfinished and we simply cannot say what, if anything, it might have had to say about marriage. It is better, I think, to say just that many of the tales are about love and marriage, and that as often as not this recurring theme serves as much to call forth divergent and contradictory ideas and opinions as it does to proceed toward a reasoned conclusion.

Dame Alice of Bath is already in full cry as Fragment III opens, and to modern readers especially, she seems to be preaching an incontestable gospel: "Experience, though noon auctoritee / Were in this world, is right ynogh for me / To speke of wo that is in mariage . . ." (III: 1–3). And her way of framing the question might well remind us of a major difference between the Knight's Tale and the Miller's: the "auctoritee" of order, status, precedence, courtly civility, as against hende Nicholas's "experience" of Alisoun in carpenter John's bedroom.

But even the modern reader must at least blink once or twice when, ten lines later, the Wife is perfectly ready to argue with Jesus Christ:

> Herkne eek, lo, which a sharp word for the nones.
> Biside a welle, Jhesus, God and man,
> Spak in repreeve of the Samaritan:
> "Thou hast yhad fyve housbondes," quod he,
> "And that ilke man that now hath thee
> Is noght thyn housbonde," thus seyde he certeyn.
> What that he mente therby, I kan nat seyn,
> But that I axe, why that the fifthe man
> Was noon housbonde tò the Samaritan?
> (III:14–22)

Whatever may be our admiration for Alice's determination in her individual womanhood, we must also feel something of the outrageousness of her insistence on it despite all evidence to the contrary, from the Son of God on down.

In the first fragment of the *Canterbury Tales,* we learned to listen for the different expressions of human love that proceed from different individuals at different points on the social spectrum. In the process, some moral and social issues much larger than the characters themselves began to emerge. Alice of Bath, as far as we can tell from the unconnected beginning of her tale, is neither reacting to any other pilgrim nor raising anything she or we might think of as a social issue. Nevertheless, she raises to a new level essentially the same moral and social issues, simply by pitting her own personal sexuality (and all the considerable wit and cunning she brings along with it) against any constraint, any order, any "auctoritee," that might be brought against it, from whatever direction.

We must not forget that in her prologue, Alice takes on not only her husbands—not even primarily her husbands—but the whole ordered tradition of religious and social authority that would pretend to restrain her individual sense of her own womanhood. Without taking sides on the matter, we have to see that in our time, as well as in Chaucer's, that is a position that will infuriate a large segment of the populace. Once again, we are involved in the divergence of views, the multiciplicity of voices, offered in the broken fragments of the *Canterbury Tales*. But Chaucer manages that polyphony rather differently with the Wife of Bath. She attracts and outrages us pretty much by herself, although the Clerk of Oxford takes a rather sharp stab at her at the end of his tale.

But suppose Chaucer had given us exactly the same prologue and tale as we have for Alysoun of Bath, but described her as he describes Alisoun (after all, he did give the two women the same name) in the Miller's Tale. Surely Alysoun of Bath's feminist harangue would have grated far more harshly on both medieval and modern ears had it come from the seductive young country tease of the Miller's Tale. Instead, we get the marvelous sentimental softening, which in the end must have made even medieval readers pause long enough actually to listen to Alice of Bath's outrageous heresies. Dame Alice is not simply an irresistible young animal to be chased to the nearest corner; she is middle-aged, travel-worn, sprung in the hips. But much of the flash and vitality is still there, and it is nearly impossible for us not to feel sympathetically drawn to the faded, worldly-wise ex-beauty, fully able to defend herself (however illogically or heretically) and still willing to look for her *Rosenkavalier:*

> But, Lord Crist! whan that it remembreth me
> Upon my yowthe, and on my jolitee,
> It tikleth me aboute myn herte roote.
> Unto this day it dooth myn herte boote
> That I have had my world as in my time.
> But age, allas, that al wol envenyme,
> Hath me biraft my beaute and my pith.
> Lat go, farwell! the devel go therwith!
> The flour is goon, ther is namoor to telle;
> The bren, as I best kan, now moste I selle;
> But yet to be right myrie wol I fonde.
> (III:469–79)

The up-beat, almost delicate fairy story the Wife of Bath tells after her long, strident, startling prologue has surprised many readers, although it can fairly easily be rationalized as a gentler and far less aggressive assertion of feminine superiority. But even as she repeats the clichés of the live-happily-ever-after ending, Dame Alice drops back into the assertive voice of her prologue:

And thus they lyve unto hir lyves ende
In parfit joye; and Jhesu Crist us sende
Housbondes meeke, yonge, and fresshe abedde,
And grace t'overbyde hem that we wedde;
And eek I praye Jhesu shorte hir lyves
That wol nat be governed by hir wyves;
And olde and angry nygardes of dispence,
God sende hem soone verray pestilence!
(III:1257–64)

When the Friar responds (courteously enough) to the Wife's Tale, he plunges us immediately into another spiteful vendetta between two of the pilgrims, although the animus between him and the Summoner raises religious (or at least institutional) issues rather than the personal and social ones that divided the Reeve and the Miller: "I wol yow of a Somonour telle a game. / Pardee, ye may wel knowe by the name / That of a somonour may no good be sayd . . . (III:1279–81). And Harry Bailly, trying again to keep the party sweet and happy, comes up with a superbly ironic line that precisely articulates what we have been talking about for the last several pages: "Oure Hoost tho spak, 'A! sire, ye sholde be hende / And curteys, as a man of youre estaat; / In compaignye we wol have no debaat' " (III:1286–88). Despite the Host's wishful thinking, we have learned well before this point in the Canterbury pilgrimage that in any company of men and women such as this one, "debaat" is precisely what we are most likely to have—some of it angry and bitter, some of it subtly ironic, some of it formally logical.

The Summoner and the Friar, who apparently have no personal reasons to dislike each other, really initiate a "debaat," a "quitting" between different branches of the institutional bureaucracy of the medieval Roman Catholic Church. Many late medieval writers, like Chaucer, saw that bureaucracy as overelaborate, self-important, and far too blind to fraud and corruption within its own ranks. The orders of friars, and those lay employees of canonical courts like the Summoner and the Pardoner, were particular targets of the reformers' moral indignation, and Chaucer here is in a way using a comic conflict to raise one of the most serious issues of his time.

Typically, however, Chaucer complicates our perception of the issue by embodying it in two very different and very humanly imaginable characters. The fat, cheerful, extroverted Friar Huberd, with his considerable charm and social grace, we know to be as big a fraud as the Summoner. But neither we nor, apparently, any of the pilgrims is angered, frightened, or offended by him. It is very easy, with Friar Huberd, to follow the church's injunction to loathe the sin and love the man. But the bullying, spiteful, hard-drinking Summoner, with a face that frightened little children, seems as ugly as the vices he practices and so he seems as damnable as they are.

With the opening of Fragment IV, the Clerk of Oxford returns us to the marriage question, or rather to the question of the subjugation of women. But in the dialogue between the Host and the Clerk that opens the fragment, the question of style, and the relation of writers to their audiences, surfaces again—as it does briefly in several of the linking passages between tales. In Fragment VII, which we will come to later, it is possible to make a case that, just as in Kittredge's notion of a "marriage group," we have a group centered on the art of fiction—the nature and processes of storytelling. Here in Fragment IV, the matter is broached by the pretentious Host, showing off his knowledge of matters poetical while good-humoredly needling the Oxford scholar:

> Telle us som murie thyng of aventures.
> Youre termes, youre colours, and youre figures,
> Keepe hem in stoor til so be that ye endite
> Heigh style, as whan that men to kynges write.
> Speketh so pleyn at this tyme, we yow preye,
> That we may understonde what ye seye.
> (IV:15–20)

The Clerk, partly simply ignoring Harry Bailly's lead-footed irony, and partly just being his naturally slightly pedantic self, answers with a self-concious allusion to Petrarch, an avant-garde recent Italian poet of whom Harry had almost certainly never heard. And then, to illustrate his command of those very skills the Host had asked him to abjure, the Clerk gives us a thumbnail structural analysis of the source of his own story of Griselda:

> But forth to tellen of this worthy man
> That taughte me this tale, as I bigan,
> I seye that first with heigh stile he enditeth,
> Er he the body of his tale writeth,
> A prohemye, in the which discryveth he

Pemond, and of Saluces the contree,
And speketh of Apennyn, the hilles hye,
That been the boundes of West Lumbardye,
And of Mount Vesulus in special,
Where as the Poo out of a welle smal
Taketh his firste spryngyng and his sours,
That estward ay encresseth in his cours
To Emele-ward, to Ferrare, and Venyse;
The which a long thyng were to devyse.
(IV:39–52)

The tale he tells of the incredibly patient Griselda is certainly one of the hardest of the *Canterbury Tales* for modern readers to come to terms with. The incredibly patient Griselda's total unquestioning submission to the inhuman whims of her husband, Duke Walter, makes it all but impossible for us to follow the story sympathetically, even on some kind of folk-myth level. The Clerk himself, at the end of the tale, seems to be trying to tell us that perhaps Griselda is not any possible model of human behavior, but rather an extremely exaggerated metaphor for a very abstract virtue:

This storie is seyd, nat for that wyves sholde
Folwen Grisilde as in humylitee,
For it were importable, though they wolde;
But for that every wight, in his degree,
Sholde be constant in adversitee
As was Grisilde; therfore Petrak writeth
This storie, which with heigh stile he enditeth.

For, sith a womman was so pacient
Unto a mortal man, wel moore us oghte
Receyven al in gree that God us sent;
For greet skile is, he preeve that he wroghte.
But he ne tempteth no man that he boghte,
As seith Seint Jame, if ye his pistle rede;
He preeveth folk al day, it is no drede.
(IV:1142–55)

That seems to remove the story altogether from any possible marriage debate, and relocate it as a kind of symbolic *exemplum* of Christian fortitude. And it is worth noting that the Clerk tells this tale in rhyme royal stanzas, rather than the normal rhymed couplets. In so doing, he associates the story with those of the Man of Law, the Prioress, and the Second Nun—all in rhyme royal, all very unrealistic and elaborately stylized, and all focused on the Christian devotion and fortitude of saints or near-saints.

Still, at the end of his tale, the Clerk cannot resist an ironic thrust at the Wife of Bath, indicating that in the back of his mind he had somehow intended to counter her heretical feminism:

> But o word, lordynges, herkneth er I go:
> It were ful hard to fynde now-a-dayes
> In al a toun Grisildis thre or two;
> For if that they were put to swiche assayes,
> The gold of hem hath now so badde alayes
> With bras, that thogh the coyne be fair at yë,
> It wolde rather breste a-two than plye.
>
> For which heere, for the Wyves love of Bathe—
> Whos lyf and al hire secte God mayntene
> In heigh maistrie, and elles were it scathe—
> I wol with lusty herte, fressh and grene,
> Seyn yow a song to glade yow, I wene . . .
> (IV:1163–74)

And Harry Bailly certainly took it as a kind of admonition to wives:

> Oure Hooste seyde, and swoor, "By Goddes bones,
> Me were levere than a barel ale
> My wyf at hoom had herd this legende ones!
> This is a gentil tale for the nones,
> As to my purpos, wiste ye my wille . . .
> (IV:1212[b]–1212[f])

It is evident from his opening words that the Merchant, whose tale follows, has marriage very much on his mind. He is, in fact, so nearly obsessed with his own disastrous marriage that he has obviously soured on the whole institution:

> "Wepyng and waylyng, care and oother sorwe
> I knowe ynogh, on even and a-morwe,"
> Quod the Marchant, "and so doon other mo
> That wedded been, I trowe that it be so,

> For wel I woot it fareth so with me.
> I have a wyf, the worste that may be;
> For thogh the feend to hire ycoupled were,
> She wolde hym overmacche, I dar wel swere."
> (IV:1213–20)

His tale, at the same time one of the bitterest and most polished and tightly constructed of the tales, puts so exaggerated a case that it is surely less a tirade against marriage than against foolish old men, the conventional *senex amans* (dirty old man) of medieval moral homilies. In the mixture of this homiletic convention with the fabliauxlike episode of May and Squire Damian making love in the pear tree and the almost lighthearted neoclassical business with Pluto and Proserpina, Chaucer manages to introduce enough moral irony, as well as aesthetic complication, into the tale to remove it a long way from the simplistic homily against senile regression it seemed to start out to be.

Fragment V opens with the Squire's Tale, a rambling, unfocused romance that starts out as though it is going to be one of those "marvels of the mysterious East" stories that had become very popular by Chaucer's time, partly as a result of tales brought back by Crusaders and partly connected with the semifictitious travel literature of the Polos, John Mandeville, and others. But it is not only unfinished; the story has not yet really begun when it breaks off after 672 lines. It is nearly impossible to guess how the Squire's Tale might fit into any conjectural thematic, stylistic, or generic associational patterns that might structure the *Canterbury Tales*.

The following Franklin's Tale, however, has long been one of the centers of critical attention in the *Canterbury Tales,* and (as noted above) Kittredge thought it Chaucer's definition of an ideal marriage, with which he meant to resolve the "marriage debate." However, we ought to note, before getting into the tale of Dorigen and Arviragus, that at the beginning of his tale the Franklin once again raises for us the question of the storyteller's artifice; his sources, the conventional genres that structure his work, the audience, and the stylistic decorations he gives it:

> Thise olde gentil Britouns in hir dayes
> Of diverse adventures maden layes,
> Rymeyed in hir firste Briton tonge;

Which layes with hir instrumentz they songe,
Or elles redden hem for hir plesaunce,
And oon of hem have I in remembraunce,
Which I shal seyn with good wyl as I kan.
But, sires, by cause I am a burel man,
At my bigynning first I yow biseche,
Have me excused of my rude speche.
I lerned nevere rethorik, certeyn;
Thyng that I speke, it moot be bare and pleyn.
I sleep never on the Mount of Pernaso,
Ne lerned Marcus Tullius Scithero.
Colours ne knowe I none, withouten drede,
But swiche colours as growen in the mede,
Or elles swiche as men dye or peynte.
Colours of rethorik been to me queynte;
My spirit feeleth noght of swich mateere.
But if yow list, my tale shul ye heere.
(V:709–28)

That is, the Franklin has been reading some lyrical French (or Breton—a Celtic language closely related to the Welsh and Cornish of Chaucer's time) stories that were read out, sometimes to instrumental accompaniment "for the pleasure" of the audience. Then, sharing the partly spurious humility of several of the other pilgrims, he declines to compete, in his own retelling of the story, with the stylistic graces of his source. As might be expected by now, after the disclaimer he tells one of the more elaborately and gracefully decorated of the tales.

The story is, indeed, about the testing of an apparently ideal marriage:

Of his free wyl he swoor hire as a knyght
That nevere in al his lyf he, day ne nyght,
Ne sholde upon hym take no maistrie
Agayn hir wyl, ne kithe hire jalousie,
But hire obeye, and folwe hir wyl in al,
As any lovere to his lady shal,
Save that the name of soveraynetee,
That wolde he have for shame of his degree.
She thanked hym, and with ful greet humblesse
She seyde, "Sire, sith of youre gentilesse
Ye profre me to have so large a reyne,

> Ne wolde nevere God bitwixe us tweyne,
> As in my gilt, were outher werre or stryf.
> Sire, I wol be your humble trewe wyf. . . ."
> (V:745–58)

But the manner of the testing is strangely artificial, and the more the story progresses, the more it comes to resemble those riddling games of logical evasion that characterize medieval French *demands d'amours* (poems cleverly built around some "question of love" like "who makes the better lover, a blind man or a priest") and some courses in twentieth-century law schools.

Arviragus, with a commitment to "trouthe" that must have seemed exiguous even to Chaucer's contemporaries, holds his wife to a promise no feudal court would ever have held anyone to. When she agreed (almost distractedly) to make love to Aurelius if he removed all the rocks from the Brittany coast, both of them knew perfectly well it was impossible; therefore no real contract. But as we should expect in a story which is by its very genre half fairy tale, Aurelius is so impressed by Arviragus's stiff-necked "honour" that he releases Dorigen from a promise in which he knew he had swindled her, and even the phony magician Aurelius had hired cancels Aurelius's bill. What exactly about love and marriage has been tested or concluded here remains as unclear as it is hotly contested among the critics. The tale ends with the Franklin reducing its *sentence* to one of those logic-chopping *demands d'amours:*

> Lordynges, this question, thanne, wol I aske now,
> Which was the mooste fre, as thynketh yow?
> Now telleth me, er that ye ferther wende.
> I kan namoore; my tale is at an ende.
> (V:1621–24)

The Pardoner's Prologue and Tale, in Fragment VI, pick up again the issue of corrupt and vicious people in what are supposed to be holy offices, and the overelaborated bureaucracy that seems to protect them. But with the Pardoner, we get still another view of the matter—another highly individualized character who manages to redefine several issues for us.

Although his is only 164 lines long, the Pardoner's Prologue in Fragment VI in some ways works much like the Wife of Bath's. It too develops further the character we had seen in the General Prologue and in the process generates social and moral questions much larger than the psychological ones it began with. But the ambiguity of our response to the Pardoner is finally very different from that of the Wife. The Pardoner has no illusions about his own character, nor do we ever generate any sympathy for him. Yet both the shameless confession of his prologue and the compelling story he tells confirm what the narrator had told us sarcastically in the General Prologue: "He was in chirche a noble ecclesiaste." Now the Pardoner, as a lay employee of the ecclesiastical courts, had no business preaching or collecting offerings at all. Still, he was an enormously effective preacher and the sermon he delivers as his tale confirms the fact. We have to believe him when he says,

> Thus kan I preche agayn that same vice
> Which that I use, and that is avarice.
> But though myself be gilty in that synne,
> Yet kan I maken oother folk to twynne
> From avarice, and soore to repente.
> (VI:427–31)

We sense another complex pattern starting to develop. There is one other preacher on the pilgrimage, the Parson, and he is as long-sufferingly virtuous as the Pardoner is criminally vicious. Yet the Pardoner preaches a highly effective sermon, while the Parson's, however doctrinally sound, must have put everyone to sleep. Partly what is being raised here is a question relevant in one degree or another to most of the clerical and near-clerical characters, namely, the problem of imperfect or downright evil people holding holy offices, doing God's will whether they mean to or not, while the purest and best-intentioned often fail. Partly, too, the Pardoner and the Parson raise again the question of rhetorical art, of the manipulation of language to convince others by arousing their emotions. The Pardoner is a master of this art and can make it work despite his intentions. The puritanical Parson deliberately forswears all art in his prologue, calling it distracting and deceitful. Yet it is apparent that however many souls the good Parson may win to Christ, it will not be his preaching that does the job.

That question of art, both in the sense of stylistic manipulation and in the sense of fiction—tale telling—in general is also just under the surface through much of Fragment VII. This time we have no introductory piece of frame story to orient us. The fragment simply begins with the opening lines of the story. We do not even know who the teller is until the end, when the Host identifies the Shipman by addressing him as "Sire gentil maister, gentil maryneer!" And the brief link between the Shipman's tale and the Prioress's does not raise any aesthetic questions, either. Still, we have to respond to the placement of the skillful, fast-moving, subtly plotted and characterized *fabliau* about a business man, his lascivious wife, and a lecherous priest side by side with the lyrical, highly stylized (again, Chaucer shifts to the rhyme royal stanza) saint's legend the Prioress relates—or rather nearly sings—about the "litel clergeon, seven yeer of age."

With the link between the Prioress's Tale and the pilgrim-narrator's own first tale, the aesthetic issues begin to come more sharply into focus, although rather subtly at first. Although there is a rubric (marginal notation) in the text of most manuscripts reading "Bihoold the murye wordes of the Hoost to Chaucer," it may well have been added by a later manuscript copyist. But we, and Chaucer's contemporary readers, know all along whom the Host is addressing, so that we have to smell some kind of game in the wind when the pilgrim narrator responds: "'Hooste,' quod I, 'ne beth nat yvele apayd, / For other tale certes kan I noon, / But of a rym I lerned longe agoon.' " It is almost a vaudeville turn. The great Geoffrey Chaucer will now, since he cannot think of anything else, recite one of those half-forgotten poems he, like all of us, had crammed down his throat by some diligent third-grade teacher.

Most modern readers, unfortunately, will miss much of Chaucer's joke without quite a bit of help. What we would catch fairly immediately in a parody of Longfellow or Robert Service we are likely to miss altogether in Chaucer's parody of similarly banal and oversensationalized fourteenth-century pop fiction in verse. We moderns may, of course, take some comfort in the fact that Harry Bailly does not catch on either. Baffled by the deliberately outrageous ineptness of the tale of Sir Thopas, Harry abruptly reclaims his post as literary critic and simply cuts it off in mid-ramble:

> "Namoore of this, for Goddes dignitee,"
> Quod oure Hooste, "for thou makest me
> So wery of thy verray lewednesse
> That, also wisly God my soule blesse,

Myne eres aken of thy drasty speche.
Now swich a rym the devel I biteche!
This may wel be rym dogerel," quod he.
"Why so?" quod I, "why wiltow lette me
Moore of my tale than another man,
Syn that it is the beste rym I kan?"
"By God," quod he, "for pleynly, at a word,
Thy drasty ryming is nat worth a toord!"
(VII:919–30)

However, before we leave this delightful *tour de force,* we must notice Chaucer once more playing prosodic games with us, as he had done all his life. Just as Fragment VII opened with the juxtaposition of the skillfully metered decasyllabic couplets of the Shipman's Tale with the intricate rhyme royal of the Prioress's, so the narrator's tale of Sir Thopas takes the complicated "tail-rhymed" stanza of fourteenth-century popular romance to its ultimately intricate absurdity:

Til that there cam a greet geaunt,
His name was sire Olifaunt,
A perilous man of dede.
He seyde, "Child, by Termagaunt!
But if thou prike out of myn haunt,
Anon I sle thy steede
With Mace.
Heere is the queene of Fayerye,
With harpe and pipe and symphonye,
Dwellynge in this place."
(VII:807–16)

It is very like Danny Kaye parodying Gilbert and Sullivan burlesquing nineteenth-century opera.

The narrator's response to the Host's total failure to understand is the tale of Melibee, an elaborate moral allegory in prose that is too readily understandable, nearly unreadable in its flat-footed repetitious simplicity. It may be, as some have argued, that the narrator is "quitting" the Host for his failure to appreciate a fine parody by stultifying him with an interminable homily almost antiartistic in its plodding prose; on the other hand, we have no way to know. The tale of Melibee has much in common with the Parson's sermon, with which the dying Chaucer chose to conclude what he had written of the *Canterbury Tales.* Perhaps, as again some readers have felt, Chaucer's lifelong interest in the serious religious concerns of his day simply led him to include such material as a part of what he wanted his readers to confront.

Whatever the case, the Host's literary tastes seem as gratified by the tale of Melibee as they were by those of the Merchant and the Shipman:

> Whan ended was my tale of Melibee,
> And of Prudence and hire benignytee,
> Oure Hooste seyde, "As I am feithful man,
> And by that precious corpus Madrian,
> I hadde levere than a barel ale
> "That Goodelief, My wyf, hadde herd this tale!"
> (VII:1889–94)

And still pursuing his convictions about literature and its direct and simple relation to life, he misjudges the Monk as badly as he had misjudged the narrator. Harry's ribald needling of the Monk elicits an opposite response from the narrator's ironic parody. The Monk, rather, retreats to a pedantic stuffiness much worse than the Clerk's Petrarchan pedantry at the beginning of his tale, and defines carefully for us what he takes to be the proper genre of tragedy. He then proceeds—certainly with no ironic or parodic intention whatever—to regale us with what again promises to be an interminable series of thumbnail tragedies until the Knight, this time, interrupts and shuts him off with the now-familiar complaint that what people want out of art is entertainment, not enlightenment:

> "Hoo!" quod the Knyght, "good sire, namoore of this!
> That ye han seyd is right ynough, ywis,
> And muchel moore; for litel hevynesse
> Is right ynough to muche folk, I gesse.
> I seye for me, it is greet disese,
> Whereas men han been in greet welthe and ese,
> To heeren of hire sodeyn fal, allas!"
> (VII:2767–73)

Host Harry, as we should have expected, heartily concurs, and so redirects us to the central issue of the purposes of fiction and the criteria for judging it:

> Sire Monk, namoore of this, so God yow blesse!
> Youre tale annoyeth al this compaignye.
> Swich talkyng is nat worth a boterflye,
> For therinne is ther no desport ne game.
> Wherfore, sire Monk, or daun Piers by youre name,
> I pray yow hertely telle us somewhat elles;
> For sikerly, nere clynkyng of youre belles
> That on youre bridel hange on every syde,
> By hevene knyg, that for us alle dyde,
> I sholde er this han fallen doun for sleep. . . .
> (VII:2788–97)

The Nun's Priest's Tale, which concludes this fragment, is the finest comic piece and perhaps the best of all the *Canterbury Tales.* In this case, the tale teller contributes nothing to the complexity of the pattern, since there is no portrait of any Nun's Priest in the General Prologue and he appears in none of the linking passages of the frame story until the Host calls on him to tell his tale. The tale he tells is another confirmation that, however haltingly and imperfectly we trace them out, there are themes and poetic ideas and moral and social issues recurrent in the *Canterbury Tales* that imply that they were somehow all meant to go together.

There are many marvels in the Nun's Priest's Tale, too many to detail here, but we may note a few that link it to some of what we have been discussing, particularly the matter of persuasion, the manipulation of language, and how people speak to and understand each other. This comic deflation of noble life and love by setting them among chickens is a highly literary poem. Like the tale of Sir Thopas, it is a parody, a comic inversion of an established literary form—in this case three of them at once. It is an upside-down courtly romance, it is a mock epic, and it is a beast fable with no demonstrable moral. Nearly half of the poem is taken up with a dialogue dominated by Chantecleer, which is in effect a comic reduction of a range of serious medieval discussion about interpretation: interpretation of books, interpretation of dreams, interpretation of other people's arguments. Throughout all this, Chantecleer is showing off his own command of rhetorical artifice and reminding us even while we laugh that many of the same artifices are used quite seriously and effectively elsewhere in the tales.

Pertelote starts it off by insisting at some length that the best way to interpret a bad dream like the one Chantecleer had just had is to take a strong laxative and forget the nightmare:

> "Now sire" quod she, "whan we flee fro the bemes
> For Goddes love, as taak som laxatyf.
> Up peril of my soule and of my lyf,
> I conseille yow the beste, I wol nat lye."
> (VII:2942–45)

Chantecleer, however, will have none of so straightforwardly physical a solution. His commitment to speech (indeed, it is the commitment that nearly kills him) is far too strong. And like Geffrey in the *House of Fame,* Chantecleer thinks of all the great "auctoritees" of the past as talking to him, and of himself as their interpreter:

> "Madame, quod he, "graunt mercy of youre loore.
> But nathelees, as touchyng daun Catoun,
> That hath of wysdom swich a greet renoun,
> Though that he bad no dremes for to drede.
> By God, men may in olde bookes rede
> Of many a man moore of auctoritee
> Than evere Caton was, so mot I thee."
> (VII:2970–76.

There follows a two-hundred-line monologue in which Chantecleer shows off all his rhetorical skills while explaining the difficulties of interpretation, only to end in a superbly wrong interpretation that nevertheless leads him straight into the sexual self-assertion he had been aiming at all along.

> For whan I see the beautee of youre face,
> Ye been so scarlet reed about youre yën,
> It maketh al my drede for to dyen;
> For al so siker as *In principio,*
> *Mulier est hominis confusio,*—
> Madame, the sentence of this Latyn is,
> "Womman is mannes joye and al his blis."
> For whan I feele a-nyght your softe syde,
> Al be it that I may nat on you ryde

> For that oure perche is maad so narwe, allas!
> I am so ful of joye and of solas,
> That I diffye bothe sweven and dreem.
> (VII:3160–71)

What Chantecleer shows us, finally, is that all interpretations are made by interpreters, usually for their own purposes, and usually in some kind of ultimate ignorance. The elaborate rhetoric that led him to his immediate sexual gratification with Pertelote ("He fethered Pertelote twenty tyme, / And trad hire eke as ofte er it was pryme") is exactly the same kind of mouthiness that will a hundred lines later put Chantecleer in the mouth of Daun Russell the fox, and give the Nun's Priest an opportunity to show off his own rhetorical pretensions by delivering a quasi-parody of an example offered in one of the standard medieval textbooks on the art of rhetoric, Geoffrey of Vinsauf's *Poetria Nova:*

> O destinee, that mayst nat been eschewed!
> Allas, that Chauntecleer fleigh fro the bemes!
> Allas, his wyf ne roghte nat of dremes!
> And on a Friday fil al this meschaunce.
> (VII:3338–41)

After the tale has roared through its Keystone cops chase scene at the end, the Nun's Priest announces a moral just as inapplicable as Chantecleer's translation of *"mulier hominis est confusio":* "Lo, swich it is for to be recchelees / And necligent, and trust on flaterye."

Indeed, such it is to trust "flaterye"—persuasive speech, rhetoric: Chantecleer got himself into the fox's mouth and out of it by "flaterye"; Daun Russel nearly won and then lost his chicken dinner by the same means. And in those terms, perhaps Chantecleer's translation was not so far wrong after all. Woman is man's undoing *and* (or because?) she is his "joye and al his blis." It is just that multiplicity of meaning in language and life that Chaucer's poetry always calls our attention to.

In the middle of the next fragment, Fragment VIII, as the pilgrims are apparently into the last day of their journey to Canterbury (they are some six or seven miles away from it), they are suddenly overtaken by two frantically riding horsemen:

Whan ended was the lyf of Seinte Cecile,
Er we hadde riden fully fyve mile,
At Boghtoun under Blee us gan atake
A man that clothed was in clothes blake,
And under-nethe he hadde a whyt surplys.
His hakeney, that was al pomely grys,
So swatte that it wonder was to see;
It semed as he had priked miles three.
The hors eek that his yeman rood upon
So swatte that unnethe myghte it gon.
About the peytrel stood the foom ful hye;
He was of foom al flekked as a pye.
(VIII:554–65)

Chaucer, apparently, has thought of still another way to surprise whatever expectations had begun to emerge from his broken and incomplete poem. Or perhaps it would be better to say that, still experimenting and tinkering with the machinery that he seems to design as he goes along, he hits upon a way to open to infinity what had seemed to be a closed, though almost impossibly large, structure. If the Canon and his Yeoman can overtake the pilgrims, so could any number of unpredictable travelers. The one or two or four tales from each of thirty or so pilgrims can become any number of tales or travelers Chaucer chooses to make it.

This new uncertainty is underscored when the yeoman promises the host to tell a tale revealing the fraudulent practices of his master, the alchemist Canon, and the Canon rides off in a rage, never to be heard of again. The tale the Canon's Yeoman tells, too, is unlike any of the others. It is not a fiction at all, but a confessional outpouring of the teller's experience in the alchemy racket run by the Canon. It has no known literary source; it may be the only one of the tales Chaucer simply made up out of whole cloth. At the end of it, however, the Yeoman manages to lead us back to the matter of books and traditional authority, with his discussion of the major medieval writers on alchemy and the disagreements among them, concluding:

Thanne conclude I thus, sith that God of hevene
Ne wil nat that the philosophres nevene
How that a man shal come unto this stoon,
I rede, as for the beste, lete it goon.

For whoso maketh God his adversarie,
As for to werken any thyng in contrarie
Of his wil, certes, never shal he thryve,
Though that he multiplie terme of his lyve.
And there a poynt; for ended is my tale.
(VIII:1472–80)

If we put aside now the issues raised by the pilgrims themselves, the frame story, and how they do and do not hold the poem together, we can consider this question of the literary artifice of the *Canterbury Tales* in yet a different way. Robinson's text of the *Canterbury Tales* has 19,435 lines.[5] The General Prologue and all of the surviving frame story from between the tales make up 3,471 lines. That leaves nearly 16,000 lines of narrative in twenty-three stories, which are (not only in quantitative terms) the bulk of what Chaucer left us.

If we look at the tales simply as a collection of stories, for the moment disregarding the framework around them and whatever other kinds of connections there may be between them, some interesting things appear. First, although I have already claimed that Chaucer is our greatest comic poet, and several of the best tales are comic, still fifteen of them, totaling over 11,000 lines, are straight, serious narrative. There are six purely comic tales, totaling about 3,000 lines: the Miller's Tale (668); the Reeve's Tale (404); the Summoner's Tale (586); the Shipman's Tale (434); *Sir Thopas* (206); and the Nun's Priest's Tale (626). Two tales, the Friar's and the Merchant's, are hard to count here because they fall on the borderline between serious and humorous: they are satires that use comic devices for deadly serious purposes. But even with the addition of these two tales—bringing our total count of tales up to the twenty-three represented in the manuscripts—we still have a nearly two-to-one preponderance of serious to comic tales—about 11,400 to 4,400 lines.

Furthermore, nearly every conventional type of short narrative available to Chaucer from late medieval literature appears among these twenty-three tales: romances, saint's lives, miracle stories, sermons, fables, *fabliaux,* literary parodies, satires, and one Chaucer seems to have made up on his own, the semiautobiographical confessional outpouring of the Canon's Yeoman, who overtakes the pilgrims along the road. To the end of his life, Chaucer continued to experiment with literary forms and styles, and the *Canterbury Tales* is even more a cross-section of late medieval literature than it is of fourteenth-century English life.

Interestingly, there are three generic types that appear repeatedly, and from this critical point of view seem to be the core of the *Canterbury Tales,* although as with the Prologue and frame story, we should be cautious about structural conclusions. There are four romances, four saint's lives, and four *fabliaux*—one is tempted to say four variations each on three types of love, courtly, religious, and purely physical:

Romances:

Knight's Tale (2,250)
Wife of Bath's Tale (408)
Squire's Tale (664)
Franklin's Tale (896)

Saint's Lives:

Man of Law's Tale (1,029)
Clerk's Tale (286)
Physician's Tale (286)
Second Nun's Tale (434)

Fabliaux:

Miller's Tale (668)
Reeve's Tale (404)
Summoner's Tale (586)
Shipman's Tale (434)

By line count, the romances dominate with 4,218 lines, but that is mainly because the Knight's Tale is by far the longest of all the *Canterbury Tales.* The saint's lives are next, with 2,841 lines, followed closely by the *fabliaux* with 2,092. However much the rich metaphor of the pilgrimage and our fascination with those vividly imagined pilgrims may dominate our final impression of the *Canterbury Tales,* it remains an excitingly great collection of stories, a collection the general shape of which also still intimates something of what Chaucer had decided to write.

The last we see or hear of the pilgrims,[6] they are approaching a little village just before sunset. The Host, in a puzzling remark that seems to imply the Parson's Tale was to be the last on the pilgrimage, turns to the Parson, saying:

> Lordynges everichoon,
> now lakketh us no tales mo than oon.
> Fulfilled in my sentence and my decree;
> I trowe that we han herd of ech degree;
> Almost fulfild is al myn ordinaunce.
> (X:15–19)

Although the pilgrims have evidently not yet even reached Canterbury, this is really the end of the poem, where Chaucer's fiction concludes. It may be fitting that the last we see of the pilgrims, they are still riding, as they have continued to do in the imaginations of readers for six centuries now. That late fourteenth-century sun never sets on Harry Bailly and Alice of Bath, Robin the Miller, or even the pilgrim storyteller Geoffrey Chaucer.

Notes and References

Chapter One

1. Unless otherwise noted, all references in this chapter to specific fourteenth-century records are taken from Martin M. Crow and Clair C. Olson, *Chaucer Life Records* (Austin, 1966).
2. Ibid., 18.
3. Ibid., 147.
4. *The Anonimalle Chronicle,* as quoted in D. S. Brewer's *Chaucer in his Time* (London, 1963) 54.
5. Crow and Olson, *Life Records,* 349.
6. Ibid.
7. Ibid., 369.
8. Ibid., 473.
9. Ibid., 493.

Chapter Two

1. All quotations from Chaucer are from *The Works of Geoffrey Chaucer,* ed. F. N. Robinson, 2d ed. (Boston: Houghton Mifflin, 1957). References to line numbers of each work will appear in the text.
2. Although, unlike Plato, he made sharp distinctions between rhetoric and poetry.
3. H. L. Mencken, "The American His New Puritanism," in *The Young Mencken,* ed. Carl Bode (New York: Dial Press, 1973), 370–85.
4. James J. Murphy, *Rhetoric in the Middle Ages* (Berkeley: University of California Press, 1974), 48–49.
5. In many treatises *poetria* and *rhetorica* become almost synonymous.
6. Augustine, *De doctrina Christiana,* trans. John J. Gavigan, in *The Fathers of the Church, A New Translation,* ed. Ludwig Schopp (New York: Cima Publishing Co., 1947), vol. 4.
7. The word had quite a different meaning for medieval writers, one much closer to its Latin root meaning "to carry over." They seem almost to define it as "to preserve and bring to life something from the past."
8. Boccaccio, *De genealogica deorum,* trans. C. G. Osgood, *In Boccaccio on Poetry* (New York: Liberal Arts Press, 1956), 105.
9. It is interesting, though, that his vigorous defense of writing in the vernacular was written in Latin.
10. Several of Deschamps own poems were set to music and his more famous contemporary, the poet Guillaume de Machaut, was also one of four-

teenth-century Europe's finest composers. Much of the latter's work survives and is available in modern recorded performances, including a number of his settings of his own lyric poems. However, in *L'art de dictier* Deschamps means by 'music' the sound patterns of poems.

11. *Oeuvres complètes de Eustache Deschamps,* ed. Gaston Raynaud, Société des anciens textes francais, no. 7 (Paris, 1891), 266–92.

Chapter Three

1. Even had he known of its existence, he would not have been able to read the pre-Conquest English poetry of the eighth to tenth centuries, because the language had changed so much.

2. It is an interesting speculation, no doubt unprovable, that one of Chaucer's continuing experimental interests was in turning long, grand, complex source poems into much shorter and more direct poems of a very different style and genre.

3. Again, we cannot be sure of the date; this translation is also mentioned in the Prologue to the *Legend of Good Women,* ca. 1386. Incidentally, five centuries before Chaucer, King Alfred, another English admirer of Boethius, had translated the *De consolatione* into Old English.

4. It is hard to discover what, if anything, he knew of the twelfth-century troubadour lyrics or of the two twelfth-century masters of fiction, Marie de France and Chrétien de Troyes.

5. Emile Legouis, *Geoffrey Chaucer* (Paris: Bloud, 1910).

6. Others like them, such as Oton de Granson, might be mentioned.

7. See *Works,* ed. Robinson, 812, n.

8. How much of Petrarch's ambitious Latin epic *Africa* Chaucer knew is impossible to determine.

Chapter Four

1. It is not very important to our discussion of meter and rhyme, but this kind of verse is called alliterative because most (sometimes all) of the stressed syllables begin with the same sound; notice the w's in line 7 and the b's in line 8.

2. Deguilleville's *Pelerinage de la vie humaine,* written about 1330.

3. *To Rosemounde,* ll. 17–24. This *balade* form uses stanzas of equal length (here eight lines), all ending with the same line. In all stanzas the same rhyme sounds are used for the *a, b,* and *c* rhymes.

4. It was apparently not his own original creation. We do not know when he first used it; it appears in several of these short poems, some of them presumable quite early.

Chapter Five

1. Note that he continued to leave projects unfinished throughout his career, not just in the first half of it; both the *Legend of Good Women* and the *Canterbury Tales* are unfinished.

2. I shall treat the prologue as a separate poem, which it really is. It introduces no fiction that in any way serves as a framework around and between the legends.

3. We do not know whether the duke of Lancaster commissioned the poem or whether Chaucer offered it on his own. He did maintain a long and profitable relationship with the duke.

4. *Works,* ed. Robinson, 266.

5. It is important to remember that in all Chaucer's poems the narrators are just what Chaucer chose to make them; we have no way of knowing to what extent they are autobiographical. What matters is that within these poems they are waking characters in the fictional counterpart of a real world.

6. See *Book of the Duchess* (52–56):

> And in this bok were written fables
> That clerkes had in olde tyme,
> And other poets, put in rime
> To rede, and for to be in minde,
> While men loved the lawe of kinde.

7. See especially Laurence K. Shook, "*The House of Fame,*" in *Companion to Chaucer Studies,* ed. Beryl Rowland (Toronto, 1968), 341–54.

8. In the later parts of the poem there are no references to this account, nor is any kind of subsequent use made of it.

9. She was "covered from the waist down with a cloth of fine transparent Valencian lace."

10. Among them is "Troylus," so whenever Chaucer wrote the *Parliament,* he had already discovered the story out of which he was to make his greatest poem.

11. In both the *Book of the Duchess* and the Prologue to the *Legend of Good Women* Chaucer also worked in a short lyric with a stanza pattern different from his basic one.

12. This is an interesting fact in itself, since he never returned to the legends proper after abandoning them.

13. I have followed the "G" version for the rest of the discussion.

Chapter Six

1. Whether Chaucer had read that prose introduction along with the *Filostrato* cannot be determined.

2. Boethius, *Consolation of Philosphy,* trans. Richard Green (Indianapolis: Bobbs-Merrill, 1962).

3. E. T. Donaldson, ed., *Chaucer's Poetry: An Anthology for the Modern Reader* (New York: Ronald Press, 1958), 965–80.

4. Chaucer's change in the age of Boccaccio's Pandaro, making him a generation older that Troilus and Criseyde, has important consequences throughout the poem.

5. We might note Chaucer's private joke with his readers, having Criseyde in ancient Troy reading Statius's first-century A.D. Latin poem about the siege of Thebes, and reading it in a medieval manuscript with decorated capital letters.

6. An *aubade* is a conventional French lyric type, the "dawn song" of lovers expressing their distress at having to part after a night of lovemaking.

7. Boethius, *Consolation of Philosophy,* book ii, meter 8.

8. Robert K. Root, *Chaucer's Troilus and Criseyde* (Princeton: Princeton University Press, 1926).

9. C. S. Lewis, "What Did Chaucer Really Do to Il Filostrato," *Essays and Studies* 17 (1932): 56–75.

Chapter Seven

1. *Troilus and Criseyde,* for example, survives in only twenty manuscripts, four of which are brief fragments.

2. *The Tales of Canterbury, Complete* ed. Robert A. Pratt (Boston: Houghton Mifflin, 1966).

3. Actually, based on the styles of painting and drawing, there seem to have been two artists involved in illuminating the Ellesmere Manuscript, but the point of my observation remains the same.

4. G. L. Kittredge, "Chaucer's Discussion of Marriage," *Modern Philology* 9 (1912): 435–67.

5. Some of these are prose, so my comparisons are not mathematically precise, but I am concerned only with general proportions.

6. The frame story is never resumed after the Parson's sermon and Chaucer's "retraction" after the Parson's Tale is not part of the poem at all, but seems to be the aging Chaucer speaking for himself quite outside the character of the narrator who had conducted us through the poem.

Selected Bibliography

This short list has been selected on the basis of what I think will prove helpful, stimulating, and fairly readily available to the beginning reader of Chaucer. It makes no pretense to completeness, nor to being a representative cross section of modern criticism and scholarship. I have not listed any articles from scholarly periodicals; any careful reader of the books listed here will find that they will lead him into that vast assortment of publications, and the various bibliographies and indexes that chart it in detail. But I do think these are books that will lead readers further into Chaucer's poetry and provide them much that will be useful in their own further exploration of it.

1. Chaucer's Life and Times

Brewer, Derek. *Chaucer and His World.* New York: Dodd, Mead, 1977. Introduction, for the general reader, to the social and cultural conditions of fourteenth-century England. Illustrated.

Chute, Marchette. *Geoffrey Chaucer of England.* New York: Dutton, 1946. Popular biography of Chaucer and background material on London in his day.

Coghill, Nevill. *The Poet Chaucer.* 2d ed. London: Oxford University Press, 1967. An account of Chaucer's life, concentrating heavily on life as a poet, rather than cultural background.

Crow, Martin M., and **Clair C. Olson,** eds. *Chaucer Life Records.* Oxford: Clarendon Press, 1966. Compilation of all contemporary records relevant to Chaucer's life. Many summaries of those in Latin or French.

2. Language and Versification

Baum, Paull F. *Chaucer's Verse.* Durham, N.C.: Duke University Press, 1961. Compact introduction to Chaucer's meters and stanza forms.

Davis, Norman, et al. *A Chaucer Glossary.* Oxford: Clarendon Press, 1979. Brief definitions and/or Modern English word equivalents for Chaucer's words.

Eliason, Norman E. *The Language of Chaucer's Poetry: An Appraisal of the Verse, Style and Structure. Anglistica,* no. 17. Copenhagen: Rosenkilde og Bagger, 1972. More extended discussion of the mechanics of Chaucer's poetry, with good deal of linguistic background material.

Elliott, Ralph W. V. *The World of Chaucer's Idiom: Chaucer's English.* London: Deutsch, 1974. Study of special or unusual phrases, meanings, and constructions in Chaucer's Middle English.

Mossé, Fernand. *A Handbook of Middle English.* Translated by James A. Walker. Baltimore: Johns Hopkins University Press, 1952. The standard scholarly linguistic description of Middle English; very detailed and technical.

Peters, Robert A. *Chaucer's Language.* Bellingham: Western Washington University Occasional Monographs, no. 1. Condensed and simplified introduction to Chaucer's London dialect of Middle English, intended for beginners.

Robinson, Ian. *Chaucer's Prosody: A Study of the Middle English Verse Tradition.* London: Cambridge University Press, 1971. Analysis of Chaucer's meters, with much attention to how English prosody had developed in the centuries before Chaucer.

3. Literary Sources and Background

Cummings, Hubertis M. *The Indebtedness of Chaucer's Works to the Italian Works of Boccaccio.* University of Cincinnati Studies, vol. 10, pt. 2, 1916. Reprint. New York: Haskell House, 1965. Brief but thorough discussion of all of Chaucer's borrowings from Boccaccio.

Curry, Walter C. *Chaucer and the Medieval Sciences.* 1926. Reprint. New York: Barnes & Noble, 1962. Extensive information on medieval scientific lore helpful in understanding Chaucer, including useful but unexpected "sciences" like astrology and physiognomy.

Fyler, John M. *Chaucer and Ovid.* New Haven: Yale University Press, 1979. General discussion of Ovid's influence on Chaucer, mainly in style and themes.

Hoffman, Richard L. *Ovid and the Canterbury Tales.* Philadelphia: University of Pennsylvania Press, 1967. Concerned fairly specifically with sources in Ovid for parts of the *Canterbury Tales.*

Miller, Robert P., ed. *Chaucer: Sources and Backgrounds.* New York: Oxford University Press, 1977. Excerpts and summaries of texts either illustrating the intellectual climate of the time or providing Chaucer with source material.

Shannon, Edgar F. *Chaucer and the Roman Poets.* Cambridge, Mass.: Harvard University Press, 1929. Mainly a source study, locating and identifying Chaucer's classical Latin sources.

Wimsatt, James I. *Chaucer and the French Love Poets: The Literary Background of the Book of the Duchess.* Chapel Hill, N.C., 1968. Critical discussion as well as source identification of the fourteenth-century French lyric poets who influenced Chaucer so heavily.

4. General Criticism

Baum, Paull F. *Chaucer: A Critical Appreciation.* Durham, N.C.: Duke University Press, 1958. A short book, with general discussions of the major poems. As the title implies, highly laudatory.

Brewer, Derek S., ed. *Chaucer and Chaucerians: Critical Studies in Middle English Literature.* London: Nelson, 1966. Essays by a group of leading contemporary Chaucerians on various aspects of Chaucer's poetry.

Bronson, Bertrand H. *In Search of Chaucer.* Toronto: University of Toronto Press, 1960. Argues that Chaucer meant his poems to be delivered orally to a fourteenth-century audience and that we must read them as that audience would have heard and understood them.

Burlin, Robert B. *Chaucerian Fiction.* Princeton: Princeton University Press, 1977. Attempts to classify Chaucer's fictions in three different types: "poetic," "philosophical," and "psychological."

Burrow, John A. *Ricardian Poetry: Chaucer, Gower, Langland and the Gawain Poet.* London: Routledge, 1971. Looks for common elements in the poetry of these contemporaries in an attempt to define a literary period.

Clemen, Wolfgang. *Chaucer's Early Poetry.* Translated by C. A. M. Sym. London: Methuen, 1963. A revision and enlargement of an earlier work on Chaucer's dream poems.

David, Alfred. *The Strumpet Muse: Art and Morals in Chaucer's Poetry.* Bloomington: Indiana University Press, 1976. Tries to define Chaucer's double and conflicting attraction to the erotic and the moral— the profane and the sacred.

Dempster, Germaine. *Dramatic Irony in Chaucer.* Stanford University Publications in Language and Literature, vol. 4, 1932. Reprint. New York: Humanities Press, 1959. Analysis of ways in which Chaucer's characters unwittingly reveal themselves and foreshadow the outcomes of their stories; Largely concerned with the *Canterbury Tales.*

Economou, George D., ed. *Geoffrey Chaucer: A Collection of Original Articles.* New York: McGraw-Hill. 1976. A collection of essays by various current critics on various Chaucerian topics.

Elbow, Peter. *Oppositions in Chaucer.* Middletown, Conn.: Wesleyan University Press, 1975. A small book, suggesting how Chaucer develops in some of his major works the Boethian conflict between joys and sorrows of this world, and the inexorable providential order of the universe.

Gerould, G. H. *Chaucerian Essays.* Princeton: Princeton University Press, 1952. A collection of reflections on some of the major critical problems in Chaucer's poems.

Jordan, Robert M. *Chaucer and the Shape of Creation: The Aesthetic Possibilities of Inorganic Structure.* Cambridge, Mass.: Harvard University Press, 1967. Argues that Gothic art, in particular the high Gothic cathedrals, provide an aesthetic model for Chaucer's poems.

Kittredge, George L. *Chaucer and his Poetry.* Cambridge, Mass.: Harvard University Press, 1915. Seminal study that introduced such controversial notions as that *Troilus and Criseyde* is "the first psychological novel" and that the stories in the *Canterbury Tales* are "dramatic monologues," revealing the characters of their tellers.

Lowes, John L. *Geoffrey Chaucer and the Development of his Genius.* 1934. Reprint. Bloomington: Indiana University Press, 1958. Attempts to analyze how Chaucer's imagination worked, and how it developed through his career.

Muscatine, Charles. *Chaucer and the French Tradition: A Study in Style and Meaning.* Berkeley: University of California Press, 1957. Tries to define two stylistic traditions in medieval French poetry, the "courtly" and the bourgeois-realistic, and analyze Chaucer's uses and mixtures of them.

Payne, Robert O. *The Key of Remembrance: A Study of Chaucer's Poetics.* 1963. Reprint. Westport, Conn.: Greenwood Press, 1973. Discussion of the major poems in terms of the ideas about poetry they represent, particularly their relation to medieval academic theories of rhetoric and poetry.

Rowland, Beryl, ed. *Companion to Chaucer Studies.* Rev. ed. New York: Oxford University Press, 1979. Collection of essays providing background information and selected bibliographies on Chaucer's life, times, and poetic production.

5. Studies of Individual Works

Baldwin, Ralph. *The Unity of the Canterbury Tales. Anglistica* no. 5. Copenhagen: Rosenkilde og Bagger, 1955. Argues that the *Canterbury Tales,* though incomplete, are unified in their concern with the human relationship between this world and the next.

Bennett, J. A. W. *Chaucer's Book of Fame: An Exposition of the House of Fame.* Oxford: Clarendon Press, 1968. Careful interpretative reading of *House of Fame,* and thorough résumé of scholarship and criticism of the poem to date.

———. *The Parlement of Foules: An Interpretation.* Oxford: Clarendon Press, 1957. Similar organization and intent to the preceding listing, although this book is ten years earlier, so its coverage of relevant criticism is somewhat more limited.

Bowden, Muriel. *A Commentary on the General Prologue to the Canterbury Tales.* New York: Macmillan, 1948. Background information helpful in understanding the portraits of the pilgrims.

Delany, Sheila. *Chaucer's House of Fame: The Poetics of Skeptical Fideism.* Chicago: Chicago University Press, 1972. Attempts to define Chaucer's attitudes toward basic Christian belief, as expressed in *House of Fame.*

Frank, Robert W., Jr. *Chaucer and the Legend of Good Women.* Cambridge, Mass.: Harvard University Press, 1972. One of very few extensive critical studies of the whole poem, including the legends themselves.

Gordon, Ida L. *The Double Sorrow of Troilus: A Study in Ambiguities in Troilus and Criseyde.* Oxford: Clarendon Press, 1970. Argues that the unresolved ambiguities in *Troilus and Criseyde* are a deliberate part of the poem's moral meaning.

Howard, Donald R. *The Idea of the Canterbury Tales.* Berkeley: University of California Press, 1976. Argues that the *Canterbury Tales* are "unfinished but complete"; that is, they express a comprehensive idea of the endless complexity of human life.

Kaminsky, Alice R. *Chaucer's Troilus and Criseyde and the Critics.* Athens: Ohio University Press, 1980. Tries to summarize the major modern critical responses to *Troilus and Criseyde,* and to evaluate and resolve some of them.

Kirby, Thomas A. *Chaucer's Troilus: A Study in Courtly Love.* 1940. Reprint. Gloucester, Mass.: P. Smith, 1959. Analyzes *Troilus and Criseyde* as an expression of late medieval notions of a courtly "religion of love."

Lawrence, William W. *Chaucer and the Canterbury Tales.* New York: Columbia University Press, 1950. Particularly useful survey of the state of surviving texts of the *Canterbury Tales* and their transmission.

Lumiansky, R. M. *Of Sondry Folk: The Dramatic Principle in the Canterbury Tales.* Austin: University of Texas Press, 1955. A further development of Kittredge's idea that the tales are dramatic projections of their tellers.

McAlpine, Monica E. *The Genre of Troilus and Criseyde.* Ithaca, N. Y.: Cornell University Press, 1978. Argues that *Troilus and Criseyde* is a "Boethian tragedy."

Mann, Jill. *Chaucer and Medieval Estates Satire: The Literature of Social Classes and the General Prologue to the Canterbury Tales.* London: Cambridge University Press, 1973. Discussion of how Chaucer's descriptions of the pilgrims reflect and comment on medieval ideas about social classes.

Meech, Sanford B. *Design in Chaucer's Troilus.* 1959. Reprint. New York: Greenwood Press, 1970. Extensive survey of how Chaucer remade his source materials so as to construct a new and different poem.

Owen, Charles A., Jr. *Pilgrimage and Storytelling in the Canterbury Tales: The Dialectic of "Ernest" and "Game."* Norman: University of Oklahoma Press, 1977. Argues a central tension between the serious and comic at the heart of the *Canterbury Tales,* and offers elaborate conjectures about Chaucer's changing plan for arrangement of the tales.

Richardson, Janette. *Blameth Nat Me: A Study of Imagery in Chaucer's Fabliaux.* The Hague: Mouton, 1970. Analyzes Chaucer's distinctive uses of figurative language in the *fabliaux.*

Root, Robert K. *The Book of Troilus and Criseyde.* Princeton: Princeton University Press, 1926. Actually an edition of *Troilus and Criseyde,* the book has a valuable long introduction summarizing the history of the story, Chaucer's sources, and the possible stages of his composition of the poem.

Ruggiers, Paul G. *The Art of the Canterbury Tales.* Madison: University of Wisconsin Press, 1965. Another attempt to define the essence of Chaucer's artistry in the *Canterbury Tales,* and to specify what holds them together.

Winny, James. *Chaucer's Dream-Poems.* London: Chatto & Windus, 1973. Critical observations on the dream poems, with a good deal of background information about the dream-vision convention and medieval dream theory.

Index